THE

HOME   TUTOR

for Age Group 11 plus

by

E. A. Cox, B.A.

ARTEMIS PRESS
VISION PRESS LTD.
LONDON

First published January, 1958
Decimal/Metric Edition May, 1971
Revised & retitled June, 1975
Reprinted November, 1989

ISBN 0 85478 215 X

Printed in Great Britain by Billing & Sons Ltd., Worcester

To the Parent :

There are many ways in which a child can benefit from working through a book such as this one in the home, particularly when he or she is about to leave primary school and enter a new academic environment. There may simply be a need to practice and revise what has been learnt already, and so to build up confidence. Parents and teachers may wish to test for special aptitudes and to detect areas of weakness. Your child may find the pace of work at school a little fast or not challenging enough; and there may be assessment tests to come for selection and for grading into streams.

The best help you can give your child at this important stage is to foster a habit of mental alertness. If you encourage your child to think clearly and express himself clearly during his everyday life it will help him more than any book. By teaching him to *use* his mind and his powers of reasoning you will stimulate his brain rather than tire it. But it is only fair that every child should know what *kind* of exercises are likely to be set for him, and that he should have some way of checking his progress beforehand. This book will serve that purpose.

The tests in this book and in its companion volume The Home Preparation Book are divided into groups for English, Arithmetic and General Intelligence. The first test in each group is the easiest; the standard of the last two tests in each group is that of an average 11 plus examination where these still exist. We have tried to give examples of questions of every type, but within each type endless variety is still possible, and the most valuable lesson your child can learn from this book is how to recognise a common problem in a new and unexpected form.

100 marks are given for each test, and the numbers in brackets in the answer section indicate the marks for each question or part of a question. We suggest the following time limits:

Arithmetic	1 hour
English	$\frac{3}{4}$ hour
General Paper	1 hour

We recommend, however, that if a pupil is working right through the tests he or she should work without a time limit at first, doing as much as possible without reading the hints that follow each paper. Then the hints should be read, work already done revised where necessary and remaining answers written with the help of the hints. Finally the result should be checked with the answer section and marked up, and for every mistake the appropriate hint should be consulted once more. The last papers in each section should be done in slightly less than the given time.

Sometimes it is a good idea to let your child explain afterwards *verbally* his reasons for giving a certain answer (especially a wrong one) or the way he dealt with a problem. Explaining a correct solution is good practice at putting into words something one knows; explaining how a mistake was arrived at will probably lead the child to discover the source of error without help.

To the Pupil:

Soon you may be taking an examination, or you may be given a number of tests in the classroom. You will want to do as well as you can. This book can help you, and so can your teachers and parents; but no-one can do the *learning* and the *thinking* for you. That is something everyone must do for himself.

Here are some points worth remembering:

1. Learn your multiplication tables; learn by heart the figures on the next page. Without them you will be like a carpenter without nails.

2. Read all questions at least twice (never once only).

3. Do EXACTLY as the questions say, especially in the General Tests. Teachers will want to see not only how clever you are, but also how well you can follow instructions.

4. Do as much as you can in every test before reading the hints. When you have read the hints, try to do more and see whether what you have already written agrees with the hints.

5. Set out all work very neatly.

6. Train yourself to work against a time limit. Do the easiest things first, and do not let yourself get stuck on one hard question. You can always come back to it at the end if there is time left. The time limit is part of the game.

7. When you have made a mistake, never be content until you have found out where you went wrong.

One more thing: when the time comes and you are taking your examination remember that nobody expects you to get *everything* right. It is what you do *before* that day that counts. Once you are there, keep perfectly calm, and do your best. That is all anyone can ask.

Length

1 kilometre (km)	=	1000 metres (m)
1 metre	=	100 centimetres (cm)
1 centimetre	=	10 millimetres (mm)

Volume

1 cubic metre	=	1000 litres = 10 hectolitres
1 litre	=	1000 cubic centimetres
		or millilitres (ml)

Weight

1 tonne	=	1000 kilogrammes (kg)
1 kg	=	1000 grammes (g)
	=	the weight of 1 litre of water

Money

£1	=	100 new pence
1p	=	£0.01
	=	2 new halfpence

Time

1 day	=	24 hours
1 hour	=	60 minutes
1 minute	=	60 seconds

Decimals

0.1	=	1/10	0.25	=	1/4
0.125	=	1/8	0.5	=	1/2
0.2	=	1/5	0.75	=	3/4

ENGLISH TEST 1

1. (a) A young cat is called a kitten. Write down what we call—

   a young dog   a young horse   a young duck

   (b) Write down one word which means the same as each of these words:— RICH. SECURE. STIFF.

   (c) Make up a short sentence, about anything you like, which brings in the word TWO and also the word TOO. Try not to use the word AND in your sentence.

   (d) Here is a sentence in which the capital letters, commas and punctuation marks have been left out. Write out the sentence again putting them in:—

   norah said no i cant come

2. Choose one word from the list to complete each sentence:—

   VIVACIOUS   OBSTINATE   PATRIOTIC
   PESSIMISTIC   ODIOUS

   (a) Someone who is always willing to help his country is . . . .

   (b) Someone who refuses to change his mind is . . . .

   (c) Someone who always behaves unpleasantly is . . . .

   (d) Someone who is lively and active is . . . .

   (e) Someone who looks on the bad side of things is . . . .

3. Change the following sentences into the plural number:—

   (*a*) The lady was lifting her very heavy box.

   (*b*) The man-servant was serving his master's meal.

   (*c*) "I am playing with my pet deer," said the boy.

   (*d*) The man's cap was blown off in the storm.

   (*e*) The fire was burning brightly.

4. Below are five pairs of sentences. Join each pair into one sentence, using one of these words each time:—

   WHO   WHOM   WHOSE   WHICH

   (*a*) Mr. and Mrs. Jones are Welsh. Their son is called Owen.

   (*b*) Jack, my best friend, is in hospital. I have known him for years.

   (*c*) The policeman stopped the small boy. The small boy was kicking a ball in the street.

   (*d*) The flowers were lovely. I saw them on the table.

   (*e*) We could not see the girl. We were looking for her.

5. Read this passage carefully and then answer the questions about it:

   In her own room down the passage Miss Wentworth was sitting up in her big old curtained bed, an ancient pink flannel bed-jacket round her shoulders, adding up lists of figures with the help of her account-book and pass-book. Her face in the candlelight looked haggard and old. She was badly in debt. Even with the allowance that John gave her she was in a very bad way. The little she made over her pigs, and selling her fruit and vegetables, were only drops in a bucket that had many holes in it. She put the books on her bedside table, blew out the candles and lay down, but not to sleep. She lay facing the window, watching for the moon and stars that shone out occasionally now that the rain had stopped, and when they gave their faint light she looked round her at the dim outline of the furniture. She had slept in this room since she was sixteen years old, and now she was eighty-two. She was wedded to the house and could not leave it. Things were undoubtedly in a bad way, but she would contrive somehow, as she had always contrived.

(a) What sort of bed do you think it was, and what is your reason?

(b) How long had Miss Wentworth lived in the house?

(c) Why do you think Miss Wentworth could not sleep?

(d) Do you think she was happy?

(e) Give two adjectives describing the bed.

(f) Name three articles Miss Wentworth sold.

(g) What is meant in the passage by—
   (i) She was in a very bad way.
  (ii) Were only drops in a bucket.
 (iii) She was wedded to the house.

(h) What was Miss Wentworth looking for?

(i) What words in the passage have the same meaning as: *not bright. looking worn-out. manage.*

6. Write a letter on one of the following: —

EITHER: You have accidentally broken your neighbour's window. Write a letter explaining the circumstances and showing what you intend to do.

OR: You have lost your purse containing quite a lot of money. It has been picked up by a Mr. Jones and restored to you via the police. Write a letter of thanks to the finder.

HINTS FOR ENGLISH TEST 1

2. Do not deal with the sentences in order, but choose first those words in the list of whose meaning you are certain and fit them into the right sentences. This will leave fewer sentences for those words whose meaning you know less well.

3. Change *everything* that you can into the plural. In (*b*) and (*d*) you must be careful with the placing of the apostrophes. These two examples may help you:

> each person's face is different from other persons' faces.
> each woman's face is different from other women's faces.

4. *Four* words only are given for joining *five* pairs of sentences. Obviously one at least of the given words has to be used twice.

5. The following method is the best way to answer all questions of this kind:

First read the passage fairly quickly to see what it is about. Then read it again, slowly, paying attention to details. Now look at the questions below, and write clear and simple answers. Check carefully whether the question asks you to use words that actually occur in the given passage, for instance as in (*e*). If, say, *two* words are asked for, do not try to go one better and give *three*, even if there is a third possible one. The cleverest thing you can do is to do *exactly* as the questions ask.

Always try to make your answer a complete sentence, unless just one single word is needed.

If words from the piece are given in the question, find them and read the whole sentence containing them again, to refresh your memory.

6. In writing all letters, remember the following rules:—

(i) You must put your address plainly, with all punctuation marks inserted,

    e.g.   4, High Street,
                    Staines,
                        Middlesex.

adding the postal code where necessary.

(ii) You must then add the date of writing the letter underneath the address.

(iii) Leave a gap before starting the actual letter.

(iv) Begin and end your letter correctly. If you are writing to a stranger, begin with "Dear Sir" or "Dear Madam" and end with "Yours faithfully," followed by your full name. To an acquaintance write "Dear Mr. Smith" and end with "Yours sincerely," and to a friend write "Dear Henry" and end with "Yours ever," or simply "Yours," and sign with your Christian name only. Your name should always be written on a line by itself; do not add the word "from", and do not forget the comma after "Yours sincerely" etc.

(a) In this letter, you must first tell exactly what happened, pointing out that it was pure accident, and apologising for all the trouble you have caused. You may then make an offer to pay for the damage, by asking your neighbour to have the window repaired and to send the bill to you. You end by saying again how sorry you are, and tell your neighbour that you will do your best to see that it does not happen again.

(b) In this letter, you could first thank Mr. Jones very much for finding your purse. Explain the circumstances of your losing it, pointing out that it was not carelessness, but a pure accident. You must then say how much you appreciate the honesty of Mr. Jones in returning the purse intact to the police, and then you can offer him a reasonable reward, making arrangements to send it to him, and ending with more thanks.

ENGLISH TEST 2

1. (*a*) Write out this sentence correctly, putting in the marks of punctuation, capital letters, and inverted commas, which have been left out:—

> can you lend me a suitcase no i cant replied mary

(*b*) Write out the following sentence, putting "Jack and Henry" instead of "Jack", and making it refer to yesterday instead of today. This will mean altering two or three words:—

> Jack does his work well although he goes about it in a queer way.

(*c*) In the next sentence four words have been left out. The missing words are all to be found in this group:— TO. TWO. TOO. WEAR. WHERE. WERE. THERE. THEIR. Put them in.

> The . . . . girls discussed what they should . . . . at the party if . . . . friends . . . . to invite them.

(*d*) Make up one sentence, about anything you please, which contains the word NEW and also the word KNEW. Try not to use the word AND in your sentence.

2. Rewrite this passage, putting a better word than "nice" each time. Use each new word once only.

> All the boys and girls wanted to have a nice day for their outing, when they were going by coach to a nice seaside place. But, at first, it seemed as if it might

rain, which was not nice at all, as they would not be able to see any nice views from the coach. Later the sun shone and it turned out to be a really nice afternoon. They enjoyed their day on a nice beach and then went to a nice field for tea and sports.

3. Select the correct word from those in brackets to complete the sentences:—

  (a) The tramp tried to (steel, steal) the (steel, steal) box from the bank during the (night, knight).

  (b) During the storm, the (reins, rains) caused a (leak, leek) in the roof of the old shed.

  (c) The mistress said, "All girls are to (were, wear) (their, there) blue blazers and to stand (their, there) this afternoon during the ceremony."

  (d) The judge said that the (witch, which) (would, wood) be burnt at the (steak, stake).

  (e) (hour, our) friends did the (hole, whole) journey in less than one (hour, our).

4. What do the following letters stand for?

  (a) U.N.O.   (b) C.O.D.   (c) O.H.M.S.

  (d) B.R.   (e) R.S.V.P.   (f) B.O.A.C.

5. Read the following passage carefully and then answer the following questions:—

  The window was open and small scented violets grew just outside. A blackbird was singing and the sky was clear. The firelight glinted upon the satin-smooth heads of the children, dark-brown, red-gold and silver-gilt, and warmed Daphne's cheeks, giving back to her the youth she had lost. She wore a coat that John had given her years ago to match the cabinet. It had gold dragons on it and sleeves wide enough to carry one of the little sleeve dogs who years ago had been the fashion in Pekin. John looked at her without any of his usual anxiety, his sense of failure, for her happiness at this moment was a part of this perfect hour. His love for her burned strong and joyous, and the nimbus that it set about her held the children too where they sat on the hearthrug at her feet. Orlando was also there, just on the fringe of the light. His fur was like satin and his whiskers threads of silver.

(*a*)   What time of the year do you think is referred to in the passage?

(*b*)   Give a reason for your answer in (*a*).

(*c*)   What sort of coat was Daphne wearing?

(*d*)   Who was Orlando?

(*e*)   Why was John not anxious?

(*f*)   What is the meaning in the passage of the word "nimbus"?

(*g*)   Put into your own words what is meant in the passage by: —
      (i) the fringe of the light.
      (ii) the firelight glinted.

(*h*)   What words are used in the passage to mean (i) sweetly smelling (ii) lack of success (iii) a case with drawers for keeping valuables in it.

6. Write a composition on one of the following: —

EITHER: a terrible storm.

OR: "At that moment the door of my bedroom opened slowly." Write a story beginning with this sentence.

HINTS FOR ENGLISH TEST 2

1. (*a*) Read the piece to be punctuated very carefully, deciding if there is more than one sentence. Always look for a question, and remember the question mark. Watch for a word like "can't" which must have an apostrophe inserted to denote a letter left out.

 (*d*) Be careful of the meanings of the words. "New" is an adjective and goes with a noun, but "knew" is a verb.

2. In this passage, the word "nice" has been deliberately put in but this adjective is a general one. You must choose an adjective which suits better the particular noun, e.g. a beach is usually sandy, if it is nice.

4. This is a fairly common type of question, involving knowledge of well-known abbreviations. Check carefully that the given answers fit the words you have selected for your answers.

5. As always, read the passage at least twice, the second time very carefully, and re-read each part in turn as you come to the questions on it.

6. General Rules for Compositions:—

 Always set out your compositions in paragraphs, starting each one about an inch in from the margin, thus presenting an orderly appearance. Write down first (on a separate piece of paper) as sub-headings what you intend to write about in each paragraph, always starting with a general opening and ending with a fitting conclusion. Read the subject set for a composition at least twice, and write only about what is set; do not wander from the point.

 Do not introduce conversation into composition unless it is especially asked for, nor too many names of persons into a story. Do use your imagination, but do not let it run away with you.

 A TERRIBLE STORM. In this type of composition, you are expected to *describe* something, not tell a thrilling story. You can describe a storm as you imagine it at sea, or one on land. Don't make the mistake of thinking that the bigger the storm, the better the composition! It is the way you describe it that matters.

 "At that moment the door of my bedroom opened slowly." Spend a few minutes thinking out your story before you begin to write. You have not time for a complicated story, so make it simple and not impossible, with a good and perhaps surprising ending.

ENGLISH TEST 3

1. (a) The feminine of CONDUCTOR is CONDUCTRESS. What is the feminine of: —

     PRINCE.   WAITER.   SULTAN.   FOX.

   (b) What are the plural forms of: —

     DIARY.   MOUSE.   COURT-MARTIAL.   TOMATO.

   (c) Write a short sentence, about anything you like, which contains the words WEATHER and WHETHER. Try not to use the word AND in your sentence.

   (d) The following words have more than one meaning. Write sentences to show two meanings of each that you know: — LEFT. LIGHT. RING.

2. In each of the following sentences some words have been put in brackets. Rewrite the sentences, putting one word in place of the words in brackets: —

   (a) Please come (at once).

   (b) I am (not guilty).

   (c) Yesterday I met a (native of France).

   (d) This book was given to me by the (man who wrote it).

   (e) He was despised by many people because he was a (man who hoarded his money).

   (f) The (people who attended the church) listened attentively to the sermon.

   (g) The (people who attended the concert) clapped.

   (h) Dentists can extract teeth (without causing any suffering).

3. In the following list there are six words, together with six words of opposite meaning. Arrange them in two columns, each of the six words placed by its opposite.

     EASY. LOVE. TRANSPARENT. OPAQUE. PROBABLE. WRONG. REFUSE. CORRECT. DIFFICULT. UNLIKELY. HATE. ACCEPT.

4. Rewrite these sentences, putting a suitable word into each space. At the end of each sentence, in brackets, write what part of speech your word is.

(a) The man ran . . . . down the road.

(b) We had a . . . . time at the sports.

(c) The boys had to climb . . . . the gate to get into the field.

(d) The maid . . . . a cake in the oven.

(e) John practised hard for his race, ... so he won it.

5. Read this passage carefully and then answer the questions about it:—

    One bitter February morning John Taylor stood with his brand new trunk watching the Sydney Star come into berth. His parents had come with him from Brixton, although this had meant the loss of a day's wages to the father which he could ill afford. Whenever his mother looked towards the dock she appeared cast down, but John was jubilant, because only the week before his father had found a company to engage him and at great sacrifice had bought him a uniform. John especially cherished the peaked cap with a blue star on the front.

Slowly the gangway was lowered and John, after bidding a farewell to his parents which was far more reluctant on their side than his, clambered up. He spoke respectfully to Mr. Davies, his new chief officer, a corpulent Welshman, who took him to the captain. Captain Byrne's stern looks belied him and John thought him far milder than Mr. Brown, left behind in the classroom. But if John had thought he was finished with school he was soon disillusioned, for two hours' study a night was expected of him.

This information was imparted by the person to whom he was next introduced, a boy who was to be John's fellow cadet and room mate. This boy soon ordered John to take off his new uniform and scrub their cabin floor. A little of the joy died out of John, but as he worked he stopped from time to time to cast a furtive glance at the beautiful sheath knife which had been issued with his dungarees.

(a)   What was the Sydney Star?

(b)   What job was John going to do?

(c)   Where had John been living?

(d)   Why was it a sacrifice for John's father to buy him a uniform?

(e)   Why did John's mother appear cast down?

(f)   What word shows that John liked his cap?

(g)   Why did John speak respectfully to Mr. Davies?

(h)   Who was Mr. Brown?

(i)   What did John wear to scrub the floor?

(j)   Why did John cast a "furtive" glance at his knife?

(*k*) Give another word for: —

> CORPULENT.   RELUCTANT.

(*l*) Write a few sentences describing an adventure you think John might have.

6. Write a letter on one of the following: —

> EITHER: (*a*) You have just been staying on a farm for all the summer holidays. Write a letter of thanks to the family with whom you stayed.

> OR: (*b*) Your friend has been in hospital for a month. Write a letter to cheer him (or her) up.

HINTS FOR ENGLISH TEST 3

1. (*a*) Watch the spelling of your answers, and do not add just well-known endings.

   (*b*) In the word "diary", because it ends in a "y" cut off the "y", and as the previous letter is a consonant add "ies". "Court-martial" is a difficult word, because the plural form is attached only to the noun — court.

2. In this question, make sure it is only one word in each sentence you are substituting for the underlined ones. Do not think that two words will be correct.

3. It is always best when pairing words, to write them down quickly in rough, and as you use them up, cross them off your list. Otherwise you will miss two out, or you might possibly use the same word twice.

4. This is a fairly difficult question, especially in regard to the parts of speech. In (*a*) the word must help the verb "ran", so it is an adverb. In (*b*) the word qualifies or helps the noun "time", so is an adjective. In (*c*) the word governs the noun "gate", so is a preposition. In (*d*) it is obviously a verb, as there is none in the sentence. In (*e*) it is a word joining two sentences, so it is a conjunction.

5. See Hints for English Paper 1, No. 5.

6. In Letter (*a*), say how pleased you were to stay so long, how kind it was of the family to have you all the holidays, mention the animals you know and the various activities you had on the farm, and end by hoping everyone there is well, and that you may see them again. Make up some names and an address.

   In Letter (*b*), the main purpose is to cheer your friend. Make up your mind what the situation is: are you living near him or at the same school? Then you probably know all about his illness and have perhaps visited him already. But if you live further away you have perhaps only just heard that he is in hospital. Once you have imagined the exact circumstances this should be an easy letter to write.

ENGLISH TEST 4

1. (*a*) Complete the comparisons:

   The man was as deaf as a . . . .
   The old lady was as poor as a . . . .
   The poor girl was as hungry as a . . . .

   (*b*) Make adjectives from these nouns:
   DANGER. DOUBT. BEAUTY.

   (*c*) Write three sentences in which the word DRAW is used as a noun, then as a verb, and finally again as a verb with a different meaning.

   (*d*) Imagine you have to put the following addresses on envelopes. What would you write?

   (i) mr and mrs w jones 4 high street exeter devon

   (ii) a. w. white esq manor house sibford oxfordshire

2. These animals and their homes have been mixed. Make a list of the animals and against each write the correct name of its home:—

HORSE (sty)   DOG (byre)   PIG (sett)
CHICKENS (lair)   BADGER (burrow)   FOX (fold)
COW (stable)   RABBIT (kennel)   SHEEP (coop)

3. One word can be changed in each of the following sentences to give an opposite meaning to each sentence. Find the word first, change it and then write it down as in the example:—

Example: The shopkeeper increased the price of the goods. DECREASED.

(a) The girl admitted that she was the thief.

(b) The policeman made a careful report.

(c) The man's writing was quite illegible.

(d) John preferred the latter of the two books he had read.

(e) The schoolmaster was very pleased with his pupil.

(f) The old man turned out to be a complete failure.

4. One word has been left unfinished or omitted from the following sentences. Rewrite the sentences with the correct word inserted.

(a) The girl was tired, so she went to l . . . down.

(b) "I l . . . down yesterday," said Tom.

(c) At our church last Sunday, the choir s . . . . . a new anthem.

(d) The choirboys said that they had s . . . the same hymn the previous Sunday.

(e) Neither of the boys w . . . the winner.

(*f*) The headmaster w . . . a good report for his prefect.

(*g*) The boy had . . . . his name incorrectly.

5. Read the following passage carefully and then answer the questions about it:—

How much Charlie understood of the circumstances of his mission or the contents of the letter he was to bear it would be hard to say. But at least it meant doing some service for his benefactor and getting back to his familiar and beloved London.

He suddenly reflected that it also meant riding a horse to London. Charlie did not remind his master that he had hardly ridden in his life. "What man has done, man can do"—that was all he felt about it. He was bidden to ride quickly to London, so ride quickly he would.

He went off to the stables and consulted the stablemen. Obadiah thought it a very good joke, and was for giving him old Dobbin, whose motion was unlikely to upset anyone. Charlie, however, demanded a quickly trotting steed, and insisted on getting it. He was sure he could hold on, by its mane if in no other way. Obadiah followed him out on to the highway, filling him with good advice about riding. "See thou ride *with* thy beast and not against him. Do thou whistle a tune to thy horse's going, and then match the movements to its lilt."

Charlie's chafed body turned uneasily in his bed that night, but his mind was at peace. He had not failed his master.

(a) What was Charlie asked to do?

(b) If he had not wanted to do it, what excuse could
     he well have made?

(c) What is a "benefactor"?

(d) What word in the passage tells you that Charlie
     knew how to find his way about London?

(e) What word tells you that Charlie was fond of
     London?

(f) Underline the two of the following words which
     describe Charlie particularly well:—

     STUPID.   THOUGHTFUL.   FAITHFUL.   AGILE.
     DETERMINED.   AMUSING.

(g) Who was Obadiah?

(h) Why did Charlie refuse to have Dobbin?

(i) How did Charlie think he could avoid falling off?

(j) Explain in your own words the advice Obadiah
     gave to Charlie.

(k) Charlie lived about 300 years ago. Write down
     two or three words which occur in this passage
     which are not much in use nowadays.

(l) What else is there in the passage, besides the
     actual words used, which makes you think that
     Charlie lived many years ago?

6. Write a composition on one of the following:—
     EITHER: (a) Describe an interesting holiday you
have spent recently.
     OR: (b) Describe a visit to a circus, saying
why you enjoyed it so much.

HINTS FOR ENGLISH TEST 4

1. (a) A knowledge of well-known sayings is essential here. If necessary, make up a suitable comparison yourself.

   (b) The words must be adjectives—i.e. descriptive words. Watch your spelling, and do not add mere endings to the given words, e.g. in the word "beauty", the "y" must be crossed out and the letter "i" put in before you add the ending "ful".

   (c) The word "draw" has many meanings, apart from the common one—to sketch. It is the word also used of "approach" (draw near); a pipe (draw air); salary (draw money), etc.

   (d) Many counties are seldom written in full, mainly because of the length of their names. Thus, "Oxon." for the county here mentioned is always accepted in its abbreviated form, but "Oxfordshire" is nicer.

3. Read the sentences very carefully first to discover the important word that can be changed—then think of one word in each case which means the exact opposite.

5. See Hints for English Test 1, No. 5.

6. In Composition (a) the important word is "interesting". Do not describe merely any holiday—it must be one that has interested you—perhaps a more unusual one, such as going abroad, or visiting places of historical interest on a tour.

   In Composition (b) do not devote all your efforts to the description of the circus, as you must say *why* you enjoy the visit so much. Try to recapture the atmosphere of the circus and some of the best acts, but do not make the composition a mere list of events or animals.

ENGLISH TEST 5

1. (a) The following sentences have mistakes in them. Rewrite the sentences correctly.

   (i) Me and Tom done our homework quickly.

   (ii) Between you and I, I think the first of the two pictures is best.

   (iii) None of the boys were in the classroom when the master came in.

   (b) Make up a sensible answer to the following questions, and write it down:—

   (i) When will you be going abroad?

   (ii) Why did the old lady fall over?

   (iii) How far is it from your house to the hospital?

   (c) Complete the following table, as you see it done in the example:—

I steal	I stole	I have stolen
I draw	....	....
I cry	....	....
I write	....	....
I choose	....	....
I lie (down)	....	....

   (d) Write one sentence to show the correct use of a question mark and of inverted commas.

2. Add a prefix to each of the following words to make its meaning exactly the opposite:—

   PATIENT. LEGIBLE. HAPPY. POSSIBLE. SECURE. OBEDIENT. ABLE. CORRECT. SENSE. AGREE.

3. Look at the eight words which follow. Write each one down and by its side give another word which has exactly the same sound but different spelling and meaning, as in this example—HEAR. HERE.

STAKE. PEAR. FAIN. VALE. LEAK. READ. RAZE. FAIR.

4. Punctuate the following passage, putting in all necessary capital letters and stops.

mrs smith went slowly down the road trying to think of all she needed at the grocers shop before she arrived there she met her friend mrs jones and said to her where are you going dear mrs jones said to the same shop as you i expect and they went on their way arm in arm

5. Read the following passage carefully and then answer the questions about it:—

When born Slipper weighed about ten pounds and was as helpless as a newborn kitten. For several moments she lay quiet, a ball of soft fur. Her mother, much alarmed, rested her ear against the furry mass, listening for any sign of life. Suddenly she lifted the baby in her rubbery flippers and held it close to her. Then she opened its mouth and for several minutes she breathed heavily into the little creatures throat. Within a few moments Slipper started to breathe.

For several weeks Slipper spent most of the time sleeping and eating. When taking a nap her favourite position was to lie on her side, or on her back, with her head dangling to one side, her flippers twitching as she breathed. Slipper grew rapidly, since the milk with which her mother fed her was ten times as rich as cow's milk.

Like all of her kind which are among the most graceful and fastest things that swim, Slipper was completely helpless in the water while very young. When she was a month old her mother decided that it was time she had a swimming lesson. Gripping the loose skin at the back of Slipper's neck with her mouth, she carried her to the pool, leaned over the edge and dropped her in.

(a) What do you think Slipper was?

(b) Suggest another name for her.

(c) Why was her mother much alarmed?

(d) How did Slipper spend her first weeks?

(e) What is meant by "taking a nap"?

(f) Why did the baby grow rapidly?

(g) How do you think Slipper felt when she was dropped in the water?

(h) What is meant in the extract by:

HELPLESS. FAVOURITE. DANGLING. TWITCHING.

6. Tell the story of your life imagining that you are a penny or an old motor car.

HINTS FOR ENGLISH TEST 5

1. (a)   (i) You must never use the word "me" as a subject and always start with another person's name rather than with yourself. The word "done" is wrong because you want in this sentence the ordinary past tense.

    (ii) The word "between" must be followed by an object—"you" and "me".

    (iii) The word "none" means "not one", so is followed always by a singular verb.

  (c) The other two parts of the verb required are the past tense and the past participle with the verb "have". Take great care with the verb "lie" (down), and do not confuse it with the verb "to lay something down".

3. Read the question very carefully, for it is often confused with the demand for a word which rhymes with the given word. Sometimes there may be two words for an answer, but only one is wanted.

5. Read the passage at least twice, the second time very carefully and realise it is all about one thing, "Slipper", a baby animal which is going to live a lot in the water. You will find you have to guess what Slipper was, but there are plenty of clues.

6. In this Composition, you are telling the story of your life, either as a penny or an old motor car. In the first example, you will start from the Mint and proceed via various owners to your present position. In the second example, you will come shining new from a factory, perhaps be sold to a new owner, and may even have been in an accident or two before you finally become old.

    As you are telling the story, you will have to use the pronoun "I". Do not make the composition just a list of happenings, but mention your feelings, reactions and thoughts. After all, if a penny is supposed to be able to write, it is supposed to be able to think as well; but apart from that you should keep your story as true to life as possible.

ARITHMETIC PAPER 1

1. (a) Multiply 57 by 12.
   (b) Add 37 to the difference between 75 and 52.
   (c) Add £8.79½ to 22½p.
   (d) Divide 3 285 by 9.
   (e) How many seconds are there in ¾ of an hour?
   (f) Take two square metres from a square whose sides are two metres long. How many square centimetres are left?
   (g) What are the next two numbers in the sequence
        1, 2, 4, 7, 11, ..., ...?
   (h) Arrange the following in order, beginning with the smallest:—

   $$\frac{1}{2}, \frac{4}{9}, \frac{2}{3}, \frac{13}{27}, \frac{9}{20}.$$

2. Divide £27.81 between two people so that one receives half of what the other receives. How much do you give to the one who receives more?

3. (a) Divide 66 612 by 84.
   (b) Now put down the answer to 66 612 ÷ 42.

4. In a day an office used:—49 penny stamps, 136 twopenny stamps, 27 threepenny stamps, 10 tenpenny stamps.
   What did the stamps cost?

5. A box contains 6 jars, each jar contains a quarter of a litre of jam, and jam costs 60p for a litre. How much does half a boxful cost?

6. When 372 is divided into a certain number the answer is 218 and the remainder 270. What is the number?

7. A father is 50 kg 500 g heavier than his son. They weigh together 130 kg. Find the weight of each.

8. A field is 210 metres long and 180 metres wide. If a man walks 3 metres in a second, how long will it take him to walk round the field?

9. Coal this year is dearer by one-tenth than last year, and last year it was dearer by one-tenth than the year before. Two years ago it cost 50p per sack. What does a sackful cost today?

10. (a) The total distance round a square piece of cardboard is 220 cm. Find the length of one of the four sides. Now find the area of the cardboard, giving your answer in sq. cm.

   (b) The rungs of a 21-rung ladder are 40 cm apart, and the top and bottom rungs are 30 cm from the ends. Find the length of the ladder in metres.

   (c) What number added to 30 will give a number 4 times as big as 9?

HINTS FOR ARITHMETIC PAPER 1

1. (f) Make sure you understand the difference between two square metres and a two-metre square. If in doubt, make yourself a diagram.

   (g) What are the differences between one number in the sequence and the next?

   (h) Rather than putting all the fractions on the same denominator, express them as decimal fractions.

2. Is it true that one receives one-third of the total, and the other two-thirds?

3. In (*a*) the answer is obtained either by long division or by dividing by factors (12 × 7). For (*b*) the answer already obtained will have to be doubled, for you are dividing by 42, which is exactly a half of 84, the first divisor. You will lose marks if you use long division for the second problem—you are supposed to spot the fact that there is an easier way.

6. This is a tricky question, and thought and care are needed to reason it out. The number which you start with in a long division sum is always obtained by multiplying the divisor (here 372) by the quotient or answer (here 218). If there is a remainder, that is always added on. So the answer will be 372 × 218 + 270.

7. This question always presents difficulty unless the following method is adopted. It means that a quantity—here a weight— is to be divided into two parts or shares, one share being greater than the other by the given difference. To obtain your answers in this type of sharing, use the following rule:

Subtract from the quantity to be shared (here 130 kg) the difference (here 50 kg 500 g). Divide your answer by 2—that will give you the smaller weight (of the son). Add on the difference to that answer to give you the larger weight (of the father). Your two answers can always be checked by adding the two weights found to see if the total is the original one, i.e. 130 kg.

8. The distance all round a rectangle or oblong is found by adding the length and width together and multiplying the answer by 2. Then the time for the man to walk round can be found by dividing the distance by 3, and so you get the answer in seconds. Express it in minutes and seconds.

9. Be careful: the second price increase is larger than the first one, because it amounts to one-tenth of a new, increased price.

10. (*b*) Remember this catch: if there are 21 rungs on the ladder, the number of gaps is always one less, i.e. 20, so the length of the ladder is found by multiplying 20 by 40 cm (the distance the rungs are apart) and adding on 2 × 30 cm (the distance the top and bottom rungs are from the ends).

(*c*) 4 × 9 = 36. To find the number to be added to 30 to give 36, merely subtract 30 from 36 and the answer is 6.

ARITHMETIC PAPER 2

1. (a) Divide 29 271 by 11.

   (b) Find out whether 91 365 is exactly divisible by 15 without actually doing the division.

   (c) Add 250 sq. cm, 0.75 sq. m and 0.25 sq. cm. Give your answer in square metres.

   (d) What is the smallest number which, multiplied by £1.12½, gives a whole number of pounds?

   (e) In how many different ways can you arrange three boys in a row?

   (f) Write in words: 5 407 068.

   (g) What are the prime factors of 180?

   (h) I bought ¾ kg of butter and 2 dozen eggs for 96p. If the butter is 64p per kg, how much does an egg cost?

2. Make out a grocer's bill for: 1 doz. eggs at 2½p each; 1½ kg of sugar at 8p per kg; 1 packet of cornflakes at 8p; 2 jellies at 4½p each; 300 g of cheese at £1 per kg; and ¼ kg of bacon at £0.62 per kg.

3. A householder whose yearly rent is £45 pays £1.14 in rates yearly for every £1 of his rent. If he saves £1 every week to pay his rates, how much has he left after paying?

4. Jack and John saved £2.40 between them. John saved 45p more than Jack. How much did John save?

5. (*a*) By how much is 5(7+4) greater than (5+7)4?

   (*b*) Express 10 000 s in hours, minutes, seconds.

6. How many pieces of wire, each 31 cm long, can be cut from a coil of wire containing 10 metres, and what will be the length of the piece left over?

7. A grocer buys sugar at £1.32 per 50 kg and sells it at $4\frac{1}{2}$p per kg. How much profit does he make on a quarter of a tonne?

8. Of £1 500 prize money, the 1st prize is one-half, the 2nd one-quarter and the 3rd one-fifth. The remainder is divided into 75 equal consolation prizes. What is the value of a consolation prize?

9. A man digs his allotment in 10 hours. A boy could do it in twice the time. How long should the man and boy take working together?

10. (*a*) A stack of boxes is 3 boxes wide, 4 boxes long and 5 boxes high. Each box contains 12 candles. How many candles are in the stack?

    (*b*) A cow, horse and pig cost a farmer at a market £70. The horse cost half as much as the cow and twice as much as the pig. Find the cost of each.

(*c*) Find from the measurements given in this diagram the area of the shaded part.

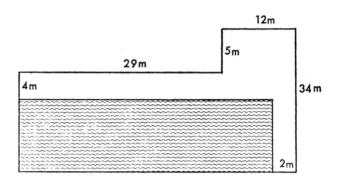

HINTS FOR ARITHMETIC PAPER 2

1. (*b*) If a whole number ends with a 0 or a 5, it is divisible by 5. If the sum of its digits is divisible by 3, the whole number is divisible by 3. Here the sum of the digits is $9 + 1 + 3 + 6 + 5 = 24$.

   (*d*) It is worth remembering that $\frac{1}{8} = 0.125$.

   (*h*) $\frac{3}{4}$ kg of butter at 64p per kg costs $\frac{3}{4} \times 64 = 48$p. Take this from the total bill of 96p, and it leaves 48p. This is the cost of 2 dozen (i.e. 24) eggs, so now you can find the cost of one egg.

2. Make out the whole bill—just finding the total is not enough

3. Multiply £1.14 by 45. The householder saves £1 per week to pay the rates, i.e. £52 per year. Subtract your first answer from £52, and that will give you how much he has left.

4. Take 45p (the difference in their savings) from £2.40. Divide the answer by 2. Add on 45p again to give £1.42½, which is the amount that John saved. You should compare this question with Question 7 in Paper 1; they are about different things but the way of solving them is the same.

5. (b) Remember your tables: 60 seconds equal 1 minute, 60 minutes equal 1 hour. So this sum means that you divide 10 000 seconds by 60, and the answer to that division by 60.

7. 1 tonne = 1 000 kg. Multiply 250 (kg) by $4\frac{1}{2}$ (p per kg). That is the total number of pence the grocer receives from selling the sugar. Subtract from this the money he spent on buying it, which is 5 × £1.32, taking care not to mix up your units. The result is his profit.

8. Find the value of the parts of the prize money. One-half equals £750. One-quarter equals £375, one-fifth equals £300. Thus the total so far equals £1 425. Therefore the remainder, which is £1 500 minus £1 425, is for 75 consolation prizes.

9. The man works twice as fast as the boy, so he is worth two boys, and two boys would take half the time that one boy would take, i.e. 10 hours. The man and the boy are worth three boys, i.e. they would work as fast together as three boys. What two boys can do in 10 hours, three boys can do in $\frac{2}{3}$ of ten hours.

10. (a) Each layer of the stack contains 3 rows of 4 boxes (or, if you like, 4 rows of 3 boxes) = 12 boxes. There are five such layers.

(b) Work out this problem using the horse as a unit. The cow will equal in value two horses, the pig half a horse. Therefore, the total for horse, cow and pig in value of horses = $1 + 2 + \frac{1}{2} = 3\frac{1}{2}$ horses. This is equal, we are told, to £70. Therefore divide £70 by 7 and multiply by 2 and we will find one horse costs £20. From this we work out that a cow is 2 × 20 = £40, and a pig = $\frac{1}{2}$ × 20 = £10. You can check your answer in a sum like this by adding the cost of the three animals together to see that your total comes to £70.

(c) This looks a complicated problem but can easily be solved. You must find the measurements of the shaded portion. The length will be the total length of the figure (which is 29 m + 12 m) less 2 m, i.e. 39 m. The breadth will be 34 m − (5 m + 4 m) = 25 m. Since the shaded figure is a rectangle, you can now find its area (in square metres) by multiplying the length by the breadth.

ARITHMETIC PAPER 3

1. (*a*) Multiply 895 by 7.
   (*b*) Add 48 to the difference between 293 and 392.
   (*c*) Divide 1 758 by 6.
   (*d*) Five children have ten nuts between them; each has at least one nut, and one has five nuts. How many have two nuts?
   (*e*) As nearly as I can measure it, the distance between two places on a map is 2.7 cm. Every cm on the map represents 800 m. What is the real distance between the two places in km?
   (*f*) Find, in square metres, the area of a field 150 metres long and 50 metres wide.
   (*g*) We have a Grandfather Clock which loses 12 minutes every day. It is put right at 9 o'clock one Sunday morning. What time does the clock say when it is really 9 o'clock next Sunday morning?
   (*h*) A litre of liquid weighs 1 640 g. How much do 375 millilitres of the liquid weigh?

2. (*a*) Change 8 357 seconds to hours, minutes, seconds.
   (*b*) Change 1 second per 30 seconds into minutes per day.

3. Three classes in a school contain 30, 37 and 33 boys. How much money will it cost to give every boy in each of these classes an Arithmetic book costing 17½p?

4. How many days are there from August 17th to December 16th, including both these dates?

5. A box of eggs weighs 3.2 kg when full and 560 g when empty. On an average an egg weighs 60 g. How many eggs does the box contain?

6. My pencil was 21 cm long when I bought it a week ago. Now its length is one-half of what it was then. What length have I used each day?

7. A man leaves X by train for Y at 8.15 a.m. and arrives back at X at 8 p.m. If the train journey takes $1\frac{3}{4}$ hours each way, how much time does he have at Y?

8. 1 000 programmes were printed for a school concert. The cost was £1.50 for the first hundred and $67\frac{1}{2}$p for each 50 after that. What was the total cost?

9. A milkman sold 0.37 of his milk in one street, 0.08 in another and 0.15 in a third. He had 96 litres left.
   (*a*) How much milk had he when he started?
   (*b*) If he served $1\frac{1}{2}$ litres at each house, how many customers did he serve?

10. (*a*) A train whose length is one-tenth of a kilometre is passing through a station, the platform of which is also one-tenth of a kilometre long. From the moment that the engine reaches the platform to the moment when the guard's van leaves the platform is 18 seconds.
      (i) How many seconds does the train take to run a kilometre?
      (ii) What is the speed of the train in km per hour?
   (*b*) A bullock costs £12 more than 4 pigs, but £12 less than 6 pigs. What does a bullock cost?
   (*c*) A boy thinks of a number, doubles it, then adds ten, then doubles what he has again and comes to 48. What number did he think of?

HINTS FOR ARITHMETIC PAPER 3

1. (*f*) The area of a rectangle equals length × breadth. **The** answer is in sq. metres.

   (*g*) Count up the number of days from 9 a.m. one Sunday to 9 a.m. the next. Total = 7 days. Multiply 12 minutes by 7 = 84 minutes. As the clock loses you must subtract 84 minutes from 9 a.m. on the second Sunday, so the answer is 7.36 a.m.

2. (*b*) 1 second per 30 seconds is one part out of 30 parts, *i.e.* 1/30 How many minutes are 1/30 of a day?

3. Find the total number of boys by adding 30, 37, 33; then multiply the answer by 17½p to give the total cost of the books. Reduce to pounds by moving the decimal point two places to the left.

4. Be careful to include both dates. Work month by month and put totals down in a column to be added up; also be careful you know exactly the number of days in a month. Thus in August, the number of days will be 31 − 17 + 1 (to include August 17th) = 15; September, 30; October, 31; November, 30; December, 16.

5. Take the weight of the box when empty (560 g) from the weight of the box and eggs, 3.2 kg. The answer will be the weight of the eggs. Divide by 60 (the weight of one egg) to find the number of eggs in the box.

6. The length of the pencil now is one-half of the original = 10.5 cm. Therefore 10.5 cm have been used in one week = 7 days. The length used per day is found by dividing 10.5 cm by 7.

7. Determine the time the man is away from X, by finding exactly how many hours and minutes there are in the period 8.15 a.m. to 8 p.m. When you have found this, take away 2 × 1¾ hours for the journey there and back. What is left is the time spent at Y.

8. The cost equals £1.50 for the first 100 programmes, leaving
   900 over. There are 18 × 50 in 900, so the cost for the second
   lot of programmes is 18 × 67½p = £12.15, so the total cost is
   £13.65.

9. Add up the decimals to give a total of 0.6. Therefore 0.4 of the
   total was left, and this amounted to 96 litres. Therefore 0.1 =
   ¼ × 96 litres = 24 litres, and the amount of milk at the beginning
   was ten times as great.

   The number of customers is found by dividing the number
   of litres sold (240 − 96) by 3/2.

10. (a) Draw a sketch map of (i) the train in its first position
    about to enter the station, (ii) the train when it has entirely
    passed through the station.

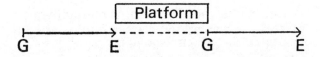

   It will be seen that if E represents the engine driver,
   he will have travelled the length of the train plus the length
   of the platform = two-tenths = one-fifth of a km altogether.
   The time is 18 seconds, so the time for the train to run a
   kilometre equals 90 seconds. There are 3 600 seconds in an
   hour, so divide 3 600 by 90 and the answer, 40, will be the
   speed of the train in km per hour.

   (b) One bullock = 4 pigs and £12; and one bullock = 6 pigs
   less £12. Adding these two results, two bullocks = 10 pigs,
   for the money cancels itself out. Thus one bullock = 5
   pigs in value. Therefore, going back to the first part, 5
   pigs are now equal to 4 pigs and £12, so one pig must
   be worth £12 and a bullock costs 4 × 12 + 12 = £60.

   (c) Do what the boy did, only do it backwards: take half of 48,
   subtract 10, take half of what is left, and you have the
   answer.

ARITHMETIC PAPER 4

1. (a) How much is $\frac{1}{2} + \frac{1}{3}$?

  (b) How much is 0.75×3?

  (c) How many grammes are there in $\frac{1}{8}$ of a kilogramme?

  (d) Find the largest whole number which divides both 42 and 182 without remainder.

  (e) $2 \times 2 \times 2$ is the cube of 2, and equals 8. Similarly $5 \times 5 \times 5 = 125$ is the cube of 5. What is the cube of 3?

  (f) Divide 72 012 by 17.

  (g) How many handkerchiefs 12 cm square can be made from a piece of cloth 60 cm by 96 cm?

  (h) Express 537 minutes in hours and minutes.

2. A full, round bottle contains enough wine to fill six glasses. How many glasses could you fill from a bottle twice as tall and twice as wide?

3. Multiply £2.74$\frac{1}{2}$ by 23.

4. Twelve different things are bought, one after another. The first costs 2p, and each of the others costs 1p more than the one bought just before it.

  (a) How much do the twelve things cost altogether?

  (b) What does the last of the twelve things cost?

5. Divide (a) 87 870 by 505

       (b) 87.87 by 5.05

       (c) 68 635 by 500

6. A man charges 22p for addressing the first 100 envelopes and 18p for every 100 afterwards. What would be the cost of sending out 2 000 notices if the printing of the notices cost 160p per thousand, the envelopes 10p for 20, and the postage 2$\frac{1}{2}$p for each?

7. A snail moves 128 cm in the first hour, becomes
tired, and during each later hour moves half as far
as during the previous hour.

   (*a*) How far will it have moved altogether at the
   end of six hours?

   (*b*) Will it ever get beyond $2 \times 128 = 256$ cm
   from its starting point if it goes on like this for
   ever?

8. A clock gains 2 seconds every $\frac{3}{4}$ hour. It is set right
at 10.30 a.m. one day. What time will it indicate
when the correct time is 4.30 p.m. the next day?

9. A path is 20 m long. At how many km per hour
does Jack walk if it takes him 45 seconds to walk up
and down the path once?

10. (*a*)   What is the area of the shaded portion of this
diagram?

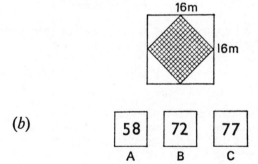

   (*b*)

   Here are three sheep-folds on a mountain:
   A, B and C. There are 58 sheep in A, 72 in B
   and 77 in C. Two of the folds are crowded and
   the shepherd wants to have the same number of
   sheep in each fold, so he takes some from C to
   B, and then others from B to A. How many
   sheep does he take from C to B? How many
   sheep does he take from B to A?

(*c*) In August a poultry-keeper found that 108.7 kg of food lasted his hens for 15 days. In September he has half as many hens again as he had in August. How long will 108.7 kg last him in September?

HINTS FOR ARITHMETIC PAPER 4

1. (*d*) $42 = 2 \times 3 \times 7$, and $182 = 2 \times 7 \times 13$. Therefore both numbers are divisible by 2 and by 7.

    (*g*) The cloth is exactly 5 handkerchiefs wide and 8 handkerchiefs long. So you can cut it into 5 rows, each row containing 8 handkerchiefs.

2. Because the bottle is round, its width is also its breadth. So it is twice as broad, twice as wide and twice as tall as the smaller bottle, and can hold $2 \times 2 \times 2 = 8$ times as much.

4. The first thing costs 2p, the second costs 3p, etc. So just add up the first twelve numbers of pence you get in this way. You will notice that the umteenth thing always costs umteen + 1 pence. So you need not go through all the twelve prices to see what the twelfth thing costs.

5. Do (*a*) by the ordinary rules of division. The correct answer is 174. For (*b*) convert both numbers to whole numbers by multiplying each by 100. It will then be noticed that this sum is almost the same as for (*a*) except that the number to be divided is ten times less, so the required answer must be ten times less, i.e. 174 divided by $10 = 17.4$.

6. Do this exercise step by step. The addressing costs $20 \times 18p$ plus an extra 4p for the first 100. The printing costs $2 \times 160p$. The envelopes cost $100 \times 10p$. The postage is 5p for 2, therefore 5 000p for 2 000, etc.

7. For (*b*), call the 256-cm mark the end, and check whether the following is true: that at the end of each hour the snail has twice as far to go to the end as it will in fact go during the next hour.

8. Find the total time from 10.30 one morning to 4.30 the after-noon of the following day. This is 30 hours. The clock gains 2 secs. every ¾ hour. This is 8 secs. every 3 hours. So total gain equals 30 divided by 3 (which is 10) multiplied by 8, which is 80 secs. Therefore, if the correct time is 4.30 p.m., the time the clock will indicate is 4.31 and 20 secs.

9. Jack walks 2×20 metres in 45 seconds, therefore $2 \times 20 \times \frac{4}{3}$ metres in $45 \times \frac{4}{3}$ seconds $= 60$ seconds, *i.e.* 1 minute. Now do the rest.

10. (*a*) The area of the shaded diamond is equal to half the area of the square, as it must be assumed that it touches the sides of the square at the mid-points. The area of the square equals $16 \times 16 = 256$ sq. metres.

(*b*) Find the total number of sheep the shepherd owns, *i.e.* $58 + 72 + 77 = 207$. He has to have the same number in each fold. This is the total divided by 3 (the number of folds), *i.e.* 207 divided by $3 = 69$. So to reduce C to this number, he must take 8 sheep from it. B is already 3 above the average, so with the 8 from C, he will eventually take 11 from B to make the 58 in A up to 69.

(*c*) The food will last 15 days in August. In September the poultry-keeper increases his hens by half the number, *i.e.* he multiplies his original number by $\frac{3}{2}$. Therefore, the same amount of food will last by inverse proportion, *i.e.* turn the fraction upside down, and it now becomes $\frac{2}{3}$ of the time. Answer then is $\frac{2}{3}$ of 15 days; how many days is that? Note that you do not have to make use of the actual weight of the food at all.

ARITHMETIC PAPER 5

1. (a) Add together 689 and 63.
   (b) Divide 4 788 by 7.
   (c) Take one-half of 38 from 28.
   (d) If sausages cost 19p per kilogramme, how much would $2\frac{1}{2}$ kg cost?
   (e) A cup holding 500 millilitres is put to catch the drip from a leaking tap and fills in $3\frac{1}{2}$ minutes. How long would the leak take to fill a sixteen-litre can?
   (f) Five boxes of chocolate, all of the same size, weigh together 11 kg 125 g. Find the weight of one of the boxes of chocolate.
   (g) A train leaves Southampton at 9.15 a.m. and arrives in London at 11.07 a.m. How many minutes did it take on the journey?
   (h) If 4 000 is divided by 9 there will be a remainder. What is the whole number nearest to 4 000 which can be divided by 9 without leaving any remainder?

2. (a) Add all the odd numbers between 32 and 40.
   (b) In a row of houses the middle house is numbered 21. What is the number of the last house?

3. A bucket holds 11 litres 25 millilitres. How many bucketfuls will be required to fill a tank holding 441 litres?

4. Margaret does $\frac{1}{8}$ of a piece of work, Jean $\frac{5}{16}$ and Ann half the remainder. What fraction of the work does Ann do?

5. Find the change out of £1 after buying all of these:

4 eggs at 27p per dozen.
¼ kg coffee at 56p per kg.
2½ kg sugar at 7p per kg.
½ kg butter at 21p per kg.
300 g bacon at 35p per kg.

6. A signalman noticed that a train travelling at 45 km.p.h. took 9 seconds to pass him. How long was the train?

7. How much is a weekly bill at a newsagent's for:

2 daily papers at 2p each; 1 evening paper at 2p; 3 Sunday papers at 3p each; 2 weekly magazines at 2½p each?

8. A man knows that a telephone number is 804 23X5Y, where X and Y stand for two different digits which he has forgotten. If Y is double X, how many numbers may he have to try to find the right one?

9. A rectangular lawn 6 m long and 5 m wide is surrounded by a paved footpath 1 m wide. How many square paving stones each side of which measures ½ m would be required to cover the path?

10. (a) A book contains 42 000 words. On an average, there are 9 words to a line and 35 lines to a page. How many pages will the book contain?

(b) An office which sends out twice as many letters as postcards one day pays £2.21 in postage. (Postage on a letter is 3p and on a postcard is 2½p). What is the cost of sending out 2 letters and 1 postcard?
        Now work out how many letters the office sent out that day.

(c) A dress is marked in a shop window at £12, this including the price of the dress and a purchase tax which has to be paid on the dress. During a sale the dress is sold at half price, but the purchase tax is not altered. The dress can now be bought for £7. How much was the purchase tax?

HINTS FOR ARITHMETIC PAPER 5

1. (h) If the remainder is 5 or more, the number you want is greater than 4 000; if the remainder is 4 or less, the number is below 4 000.

2. (a) Write down the odd numbers 33, 35, 37, 39, and then add.

    (b) It does not matter whether the houses in the row have odd numbers only or are numbered 1, 2, 3 . . . . — you do not want to know how many houses there are, but simply the number written on the last house, and this is the same in either case.

      Think about this: the middle one of 5 things is the third, but twice three does *not* make five.

4. Add Margaret's share, one-eighth, to Jean's five-sixteenths. The result is seven-sixteenths. Therefore the remainder of the work to be done is nine-sixteenths. Ann does one-half of this.

6. The train must go its own length to pass the signalman, so the question now means, how far does the train, going at 45 km.p.h., go in 9 seconds? There are 3 600 secs. in one hour (*i.e.* 400 × 9). So divide the 45 × 1 000 metres by 400 and you will get the distance which equals the length of the train.

7. This is a simple matter of adding up, but remember that the daily papers and the evening papers come out on the six week-days only, and the magazines once each during the week.

8. Remember that $2 \times 0 = 0$, but that the two missing digits must be *different*.

9. Twice $\frac{1}{2}$ m is 1 m, so the footpath is everywhere two paving stones wide. Each of the corners needs four stones, so all four corners need 16 stones. Each short side is ten stones long and two stones broad = 20 stones. Each long side is 12 stones long and two stones broad = 24 stones.

4 corners	16 stones
2 long sides	48 stones
2 short sides	40 stones
TOTAL NO. NEEDED =	104 stones.

10. (*a*) The number of words on a page = $9 \times 35 = 315$. To find the number of pages, divide the total number of words in the book, 42 000, by 315. The answer to the division is 133 and some words over; so, as it will not go exactly, allow one extra page for the remainder, although the last page is not filled completely with words. Therefore, the total number of pages = 134. By the way, can a book have an *odd* number of pages if we count blank pages?

(*b*) A group of two letters and one postcard costs $(2 \times 3p) + 2\frac{1}{2}p = 8\frac{1}{2}p$.

Taking a group to have a value of $8\frac{1}{2}p$, find the number of times that $8\frac{1}{2}p$ goes into £2.21 (converted into pence). This is 26, so it means there are 26 groups sent out that day. One group was made up of 2 letters and 1 postcard, so the total number of letters sent out is 26×2.

(*c*) The dress plus tax costs £12. Half the price of the dress plus the tax costs £7. Therefore, the difference between these two amounts, £5, is half the cost of the dress. So the dress must cost £10. The difference between this and the price on the label must be the tax.

GENERAL PAPER 1

1. (*a*) Sheila is now three years older than Janet was
a year ago. How old will Janet be when Sheila
is 16?

   (*b*) There are five trees in a row in my garden.
The oak is next to the beech, the pine is
between the larch and the oak, and the larch
is between the chestnut and the pine.

   Which tree is next but one to the larch?

   Which tree is farthest from the chestnut?

2. Copy out the words in capital letters. Then choose
one word from each line that has the same, or
nearly the same, meaning as the word in capital
letters. Write it down.

   NEAT: care, tidy, good, industrious.

   PREFACE: looks, contents, foreword,
picture.

   POSITION: place, top, bottom, middle.

   CROWD: queue, watch, army, throng.

   INCLUDE: omit, count, contain, write.

   ONE: nothing, unit, hundred, person.

   COUPLE: wedding, eyes, pair, feet.

   NEW: recent, understood, old, smart.

   SAVAGE: warrior, shark, angry, fierce.

   QUARTER: part, fourth, share, fifteen.

3. Draw a ring round the wrong answers to the following:

5 millilitres of water weigh:

5 g	$\frac{1}{20}$ kg	5 cubic cm
0.005 kg	0.5 g	$\frac{8}{400}$ kg

4. Below are 10 jumbled names of animals. Re-arrange the letters in your mind to make the animals' names and then write down the first letter of each. Thus Reed stands for Deer. The answer would be D.

(a) yemonk   (b) dread   (c) ladzir

(d) leapthen   (e) hespe   (f) figfare

(g) batrib   (h) toret   (i) lawsur

(j) ropelad

5. How many odd numbers are there between 1 and 13?

6 If you look at the first of these columns you will see how the word TIME has been changed, step by step, into the word SORT. Only one letter has been altered each time, and at each step a real word has been made.

TIME   CHAT
TIRE
TORE
SORE
SORT

In the second column, put in real words which will change the word CHAT to the word HOSE.

7. Complete the following proverbs:

    (*a*) A . . . . . in the hand is worth two in **the**
    . . . . .

    (*b*) A . . . . in time saves . . . . .

    (*c*) Too many . . . . spoil the . . . . .

    (*d*) A . . . . gathers no . . . . .

    (*e*) Out of . . . . . , out of . . . . .

8. These sums are correct, but the signs are missing.
Write the sums out and put in the correct signs.

    Example: 3 2 7 = 13:   3 × 2 + 7 = 13

(*a*)	8	3	10	=	38
(*b*)	2	12	4	=	6
(*c*)	5	7	3	=	9
(*d*)	11	6	9	=	14
(*e*)	4	5	6	=	14

9. The lines in the following paragraphs have been
printed in the wrong order. Put the figure 1 at the
end of the line which should have been first, the
figure 2 at the end of the line which should have
been second and so on:

    the Atlantic alone in a rubber
    that shipwrecked men can live
    scientist who is attempting to cross
    for a long time on fish.
    terday at three o'clock. He left his
    Dr. Alan Bombard, a French
    Tangier. He is trying to prove
    boat, sailed into Casablanca yes
    mate and navigator behind at

10. Only Mary and Alice can knit. Only Alice and Maud can cook. Only Mary and Maud can swim.

Now answer these questions, putting a tick under the name or names on the right which are correct in each case.

Alice Mary Maud No-one

(a) Who can knit
and swim?

(b) Who can knit,
cook and swim?

(c) Who can knit
and cook?

(d) Who is the only
one that swims?

(e) Who can cook
but can't knit?

HINTS TO GENERAL PAPER 1

1. (a) Sheila must be two years older than Janet is *now*, and so Janet will always be two years younger than Sheila.

(b) Draw a plan of the trees, according to the clues you are given. Begin by marking the oak next to the beech; it does not matter which you put on the left or on the right. Next, put the pine on the free side of the oak, and the larch on the other side of the pine, and so on. When the map is complete, you can simply read off the answers to the questions.

3. Draw a ring round the *wrong* answers, and do NOT put marks round the right answers.

4. If you have difficulty with one of the jumbled group of letters, write them roughly in a circle, like this:

```
        E   M
    Y         O
        K   N
```

6. By changing just one letter in chat you can make chap, char, that, chit, coat and other words, but only coat helps you here, because it already has an O in second place like hose. For the next step, try to fit an H in first place, or an S in the third, or an E in the last, and so on.

8. (a) $8 + 3 \times 10 = 8 + 30$, but $(8 + 3) \times 10 = 11 \times 10$.

9. The clue for the start is the capital letter at the beginning of a line. It must obviously be the line starting with "Dr. Alan Bombard", for the only other line beginning with a capital letter has "Tangier" followed at once by a full stop. Stress the end of a line in your mind and search for the one that links up with it and makes good sense.

10. Do this step by step, and it will be easy. For instance, for (a) first look to see who can knit: Mary and Alice. Who can swim? Mary and Maud. Who can do both? Obviously Mary can.

There is a little catch in (d). Perhaps there is not an *only* one that swims. If there are more than one, then the right answer is: "No-one is the only one that swims."

GENERAL PAPER 2

1. Each line of letters runs in a certain order. Find how the letters run and write down the four letters that would follow each line.

Example: ABXXCDXXEFXX . . . GHXX

(a) A X X C X X E X X G X X

(b) S X R X Q X P X O X N X

(c) B C X X F G X X J K X X

(d) A B X C E X F I X J N X

(e) K I X L H X M G X N F X

GENERAL INTELLIGENCE 53

2. Rearrange the following mixed sentences so as to make sense.

Capital London England the of is.
She and fell down slipped stairs the.
Girl saw bump motor-cars each two other the the.
The the and man roared fired lion his gun.
Off the bus stopped the child and got.

3. What name accurately describes each of the following groups of things? The *first* letter of each answer is given: write down the *last* letter of each. For example, each of the four things in (*k*) is a tool, so the answer would be L.

(*a*) Wales, Russia, Italy, Brazil.   C

(*b*) Mediterranean, Baltic, Atlantic, Caspian. S

(*c*) B, L, U, E.   L

(*d*) Ring, Boom, Rumble, Hoot.   S

(*e*) Boat, Vein, Cup, Ship.   V

(*f*) 1, 9, 4, 6.   F

(*g*) Arrow, sword, rifle, machine-gun.   W

(*h*) Cathedral, hotel, museum, bungalow.   B

(*i*) Orange, banana, peach, grape.   F

(*j*) Shark, herring, salmon, trout.   F

(*k*) (*Example*) spade, hammer, chisel, spanner T

4. In printing the word SCAR the printer accidentally reversed two letters which were next to one another, making it SACR. The same kind of mistake has been made in printing each of these words. In each case, write what the word should have been:

UPT.　CRON.　CAORN.　BETN.　SKEEWR.　STATINO.

5. Come home and do not bring the children until some arrangements are made to help mother. This we must do quickly.

The above passage contains a secret message which you can find as follows: leave a word, cross out one word; leave a word, cross out two, leave a word, cross out three and so on, crossing out one more word each time.

What is the message?

6. (a) What whole number is greater than 15 and smaller than 19 and also greater than 17 and smaller than 22?

(b) If Gwen gives Rose 2p the two girls would have the same amount of money. Complete this statement:

If, instead, Rose had given Gwen 2p, then Gwen would have had . . . . more than Rose.

7. A B C D E F G H I J K L M N O P Q R S T U V W X Y Z

(a) What is the third letter of the alphabet after H?

(b) What is the fifth letter of the alphabet before P?

(c) What is the fourth letter of the alphabet after the middle letter of "Price"?

(d) What letter comes halfway between N and T?

(e) Which of the letters that occur once only in "Committee Meeting" comes latest in the alphabet?

8. Find and write down the word needed to complete the analogy. It is one of the five at the end of each example.

   (*a*) AB:CD . . . FG: (AC/HI/BD/IJ/JK)

   (*b*) This:that . . . here:
(where/whence/thither/there/whither)

   (*c*) 4:9 . . . 16: (20/25/36/81/100)

   (*d*) He:man . . . she:
(girl/aunt/mother/woman/queen)

   (*e*) One:many . . . star:
(planet/sun/constellation/universe/sky)

   (*f*) Child:girl . . . parent:
(child/mother/grandfather/uncle/aunt)

   (*g*) Departure:arrival . . . go:
(leave/stop/terminus/platform/come)

   (*h*) Chop:steak . . . mutton:
(ham/pork/beef/veal/cutlet)

   (*i*) Hour:time . . . mile:
(furlong/day/distance/speed/race)

   (*j*) Soon:never . . . near:
(ever/nowhere/somewhere/distant/far/off)

9. Look at the drawing of the circle, triangle and oblong, and then answer the questions.

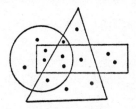

(a) How many dots are in the circle only?

(b) How many dots are in the triangle only?

(c) How many dots are in the oblong only?

(d) How many dots are in the circle and triangle but not in the oblong?

(e) How many dots are in the circle and oblong but not in the triangle?

(f) How many dots are in the oblong and triangle but not in the circle?

(g) How many dots are in the circle, triangle and oblong?

10. Look at the nine squares opposite. The numbers 1 to 9 are to be arranged in them in a certain order. Three numbers are already given. You are also given the following facts.

5 is in the first row across.

2 is in the second row across.

4 is in the third row across.

	6	
8		
		3

The totals of the columns downwards are, first column, 13; second, 15; third, 17. Now complete the squares.

HINTS TO GENERAL PAPER 2

1. You should find out the rule by which the letters in each row are arranged before trying to give the answer. It will help if you write down the whole alphabet on some scrap paper first, for counting the intervals between any two letters.

   The X's here separate the other letters, so you can think of an X as a gap. The rule for the example is then that there are the pairs AB, CD, EF, etc., with always two gaps (*i.e.* XX) between each pair and the next. Therefore the last two gaps must be followed by the next pair, which is GH, and then come the next two gaps, namely XX.

   In (*b*), the main letters run backwards, beginning with S.

   In (*c*) there is a jump of two between the last letter of one pair and the first letter of the next pair, *i.e.* after C you jump D and E and the next pair begins with F.

   In (*d*) it is the jumps between the first and last letter of each pair that get bigger every time.

   (*e*), see which letters go K, L, M, N . . . and which go F, G, H, I but backwards.

5. The message begins: "Come and bring. . . ."

6. (*a*) The first part of the question shows you that it must be 16, 17 or 18. The second part shows that it must be 18, 19, 20 or 21. Which number fulfils *both* conditions?

9. Great care must be used to study the particular figure named in each question. Thus in (*a*) only the circle is concerned. Cutting out the rest of the geometrical figures, we see only two dots are left. In (*f*) eliminate the circle dots in the oblong and those in oblong outside triangle, and only one will be left.

10. 5 may be in the first or third square in the top line. It cannot be in the first for the total downwards in that column is 13 (this would make the bottom left figure 0 which is not included in the given numbers). Therefore 5 must be in the top right square. This means that the middle right is 9 since the total down in that column is 17. 2, therefore, which we are told is in the second row across, must be in the middle square. That leaves 7 as the remainder of the second column down total. The 4 must then be put in the bottom left leaving 1 for the top left.

GENERAL PAPER 3

1. Look at the following table. It shows how many articles were sold by a jeweller during a week.

	WATCHES	RINGS	BROOCHES
Monday	2	3	2
Tuesday	4	7	5
Wednesday	7	2	3
Thursday	5	8	6
Friday	7	9	8
Saturday	8	10	7

Now answer the questions below:

(a) How many articles were sold in the week?

(b) On which day were most articles sold?

(c) How many rings and brooches were sold on Friday and Saturday?

(d) Which were sold most of in the week: rings, brooches or watches?

(e) When were fewest articles sold?

2. A foreigner who did not understand English very well made up the following words. Opposite each word, put what you think he really meant.

house-entrance
rain-avoider
time-teller
aeroplane-director
grass-scissors
fruit-field

3. Answer the following by underlining the correct answer:

(a) Is all ink black?   Yes   No   I do not know

(b) Is every chair a piece of furniture?   Yes   No   I do not know

(c) Are all cooks women?   Yes   No   I do not know

(d) Can a square have more than four sides?   Yes   No   I do not know

(e) If you were rich are you sure you would be happy?   Yes   No   I do not know

4. Here are some crossword clues with incomplete words. Give the correct word in the space opposite each. Each dot represents a letter.

P . . M   means very proper in manner.
P . . M   a fruit.
S . . E   a fish.
S . . E   certain.
P . . M   a tree.
S . . E   secure.
S . . E   satisfy.

5. Two boys, Tom and John, each have some marbles. If John gave Tom 2 marbles they would both have the same number of marbles. If Tom gave John 2, then he would have half as many as John. How many has each boy?

6. A B C D E F G H I J K L M N O P Q R S T U V W X Y Z

(a) Write down the ninth letter of the alphabet.

(b) Write down the fourth letter before S.

(*c*) Write down the letter that comes a third of the way between F and N.

(*d*) Write down the letter that comes fifth after the second letter before L.

(*e*) If K comes before J write X; if not, write the sixth letter before X.

7. If you arrange each of the following groups in order of size, which item in each group will be in the middle? Write the letter—A, B, C, D or E— not the word.

1. (*a*) rope   (*b*) cotton   (*c*) hawser
     (*d*) cord   (*e*) thread

2. (*a*) daisy   (*b*) sunflower (*c*) hollyhock
     (*d*) buttercup   (*e*) rose

3. (*a*) branch   (*b*) twig   (*c*) tree
     (*d*) bud   (*e*) trunk

4. (*a*) boy   (*b*) baby   (*c*) giant
     (*d*) youth   (*e*) man

5. (*a*) year   (*b*) minute   (*c*) second
     (*d*) month   (*e*) hour

6. (*a*) paragraph (*b*) chapter   (*c*) sentence
     (*d*) book   (*e*) word

8. Find and write down the words in the brackets that will best complete the following sentences.

(*a*) Grass is . . . (blue, yellow, red, green, grey)

(*b*) A dozen is eight . . . than a score. (over, times, less, also, more)

(*c*) To smooth a plank of wood a . . . is required. (hammer, chisel, screwdriver, saw, plane) (*d*) Before entering someone else's room you should . . . on the door.   (bang, kick, knock, slam, press)

(*e*) When you write with a pencil you cannot make . . . (mistakes, figures, blots, letters, alterations)

(*f*) The . . . days of the year are in the summer. (shortest, coldest, happiest, longest, coolest)

(*g*) Metal bars . . . when they are heated. (fall snap, expand, ring, explode)

(*h*) In very cold weather water taps often . . . (run, sag, thaw, freeze, drip)

(*i*) When snow is . . . it is usually powdery. (dry, wet, warm, moist, frozen)

(*j*) I could not get your collar stiffer. I had no . . . (soap, starch, powder, soda)

9. The table shows the marks of eight children in four subjects at a test.

	ENGLISH	ARITHMETIC	HISTORY	GEOGRAPHY
MARY	8	7	9	7
JOAN	6	8	6	6
SUSAN	8	9	8	7
DORIS	4	6	4	6
JACK	5	–	7	9
FRANK	9	7	5	4
PETER	7	10	8	6
IAN	5	9	6	7

Answer these questions:

(*a*) Who got top marks in arithmetic?

(*b*) Who got top marks in geography?

(*c*) Who got most marks for the whole of the test?

(*d*) Who got fewest marks for the whole of the test?

(*e*)   Who was second in all four subjects ?

(*f*)   Which two children got the same total marks ?

(*g*)   Which test did Jack miss ?

10. At numbers 1, 3, 5, 7, and 9, King Street live Fred, Tom, George, Bert, Arthur, but not in this order. Their surnames are Smith, Jones, Farrar, Brown, Ambler, but again not in order. Their occupations, once more not in order, are Furrier, Solicitor, Plumber, Merchant and Auctioneer.

    One of them has the same first letter for his Christian name, surname and profession, and another has the same first letter for these three things and for the number of his house as well. One of these two lives at number 9.

    Smith lives at an end house. George lives next door but one to Fred. Tom Brown lives next door to the plumber. Bert is the merchant.

    Write out the numbers of the houses, their occupants' full names and occupations.

HINTS TO GENERAL PAPER 3

5. Tom obviously has four fewer marbles than John at the beginning (twice the 2 given). Then, if Tom gave John two, he would have 8 less than John—this is half as many as John then has, we are told, so 8 represents a half of John's total then. Therefore, John has 16, which is made up of his original number plus two given by Tom. So John has 14 and Tom 10.

7. You may make the arrangement in order of size in two ways, ascending or descending. It is essential that the first word you select is the smallest or largest, e.g. in (5) it is either SECOND (smallest) or YEAR (largest). Each selection gives HOUR as the middle word, and so the answer is E.

10. This is an "inference" question, where all the clues are given in the statements. They must be sorted out gradually. Draw

columns for the number of the houses, two for the names
and the fourth for occupations. The main clue is "one of
them has the same first letter for these three things and for
the number of his house". This must be F for No. 5.

GENERAL PAPER 4

1. Look at each list of five things below and see if you
   can find the one that belongs to a different sort of
   group from the others. Write it down.
   (a) Elm, oak, tulip, ash, poplar
   (b) hat, coat, trousers, umbrella, scarf
   (c) red, blue, green, yellow, paper
   (d) sit, stand, walk,˙ride, run
   (e) ham, mutton, beef, lard, pork
   (f) potato, apple, pear, plum, peach
   (g) salmon, cod, crab, plaice, herring
   (h) trumpet, violin, bugler, flute, guitar

2. If you leave L out of FLAVOUR you get the word
   FAVOUR. What letter can be taken from each of
   the following words to leave a different word?
   (a) PRESIDENT   (b) TROPICAL   (c) THOROUGH
   (d) PALMER   (e) WREATH   (f) BUNGLE
   (g) ROTATING   (h) WINDOW   (i) FEATHER
   (j) SLAUGHTER

3. The police know that the man who stole the dia-
   monds was dark, well-dressed, left-handed, smoked
   a pipe and wore a signet ring.
         The suspects are A, B, C, D, E, F.
         All are smokers. E is shabby and left-handed.
         A and B smoke cigarettes only. Only A, C,
   and D wear rings.
         A, C, and E are dark. D is right-handed.
   Who is the thief?

4. What two numbers should come next on each line?

   (*a*) 1, 2, 4, 8, 16, 32 . . . .

   (*b*) 1, 8, 15, 22, 29, 36 . . . .

   (*c*) 63, 58, 53, 48, 43, 38 . . . .

   (*d*) 2, 3, 5, 8, 12, 17 . . . .

   (*e*) 8, 9, 7, 10, 6, 11 . . . .

   (*f*) 3, 9, 27, 81, 243 . . . .

   (*g*) 12, 9, 13, 8, 14, 7 . . . .

   (*h*) 5, 8, 8, 12, 12, 17 . . . .

5. On Monday I walked half as far as I walked on Sunday. On Tuesday I walked half as far again as I walked on Monday. On which day did I walk farthest?

6. Put one suitable word in each gap in the following:
   My aunt, who married my . . . . . George five years ago, lives in a small . . . . . in the country. We go to . . . . . with her every summer. We look . . . . . eagerly to our visit, for my aunt is an . . . . . hostess and does everything in her power to make us . . . . . at home. In return we help her to . . . . . the house, ... the ducks and . . . . . the lawn.

7. (*a*) Write down the letter that occurs most often in INSINCERITY.

   (*b*) Write down a five-letter word in INSINCERITY.

   (*c*) Which two days of the week have the same second letter?

   (*d*) Which three days of the week have the same number of letters?

   (*e*) Write down the first and last letters of the month that has six letters.

8. The items in each of the following questions can be re-arranged to form a certain order. When you have arranged them in your mind, write down the first and last in the new order.

(a) Paris, Whitehall, Australia, Middle East, Spain.

(b) good, poor, very good, excellent, fair

(c) bucket, cup, egg-cup, reservoir, tank

(d)

(e)

(f) week, hour, year, month, day

9. Read the following letter:

24, High Street,
Epton.
Sunday, April 28th.

Dear John,

You left your overcoat here last Friday. Perhaps you will call for it when you pass this way next Wednesday. I shall be going away next Friday.

Your sincerely,
Peter.

(a) What was the date when the overcoat was left behind? (April 22nd, 23rd, 24th, 25th, 26th, 27th.)

(b) Give the date when John was expected to call for his overcoat.
(April 28th, 29th, 30th, May 1st, 2nd, 3rd, 4th.)

(c) On what date will Peter be going away? (May 1st, 2nd, 3rd, 4th, 5th, 6th.)

(*d*) In the year when the note was written, on which day of the week did May begin?

(*e*) For how many days did Peter expect the overcoat to remain at his house?

10. Brown is tall and dark. Smith is tall and fair. Jones is small and dark. White is small and fair. Green, medium size, dislikes Smith and Jones but likes Brown and White.

These five men ran a race.

A tall man won and a small man was last.

Green was glad he came in front of the men he disliked. Jones was fourth. What was the order in which they finished the race?

HINTS TO GENERAL PAPER 4

2. Check each word carefully. Some answers will be obvious at a glance, but if any word gives you difficulty, try leaving out one letter at a time until a real word is left.

3. This is an "inference" question, and the answer is best found by eliminating the innocent suspects. First write down the names of all the men, A, B, C, D, E and F. The thief smoked a pipe, so A and B are not guilty as they smoke only cigarettes, and you can cross them off. The thief wore a ring, and so do A, C, D, but A has already been eliminated, so that you are left with C and D. But D is right-handed, whereas the thief was left-handed. This leaves only one suspect.

4. This very common type of question is solved only by working out how each series runs. First check whether it is ascending or descending, *i.e.* whether it goes up or down. If ascending, it is probably formed either by adding on certain numbers or multiplying by a fixed number; if descending, by subtracting or dividing. Sometimes the numbers may be grouped in pairs, with something different happening to each number in the group.

In (*a*) you are multiplying by two; (*b*) adding 7; (*c*) subtracting 5; (*d*) adding 1, then adding 2, then adding 3, etc. In (*e*) the numbers must be grouped in pairs: the first number in each pair always goes down by 1 starting from 8, and the second number in each pair always goes up by 1 starting with 9. In (*f*) you multiply by 3. In (*g*) we have pairs again, the first number in each pair always increasing by one while the second decreases. The rule for (*h*) is: add 3, repeat the last number, add 4, repeat, add 5, and so on.

5. You can easily do this by saying to yourself: "Suppose I walked one mile on Sunday; then how far did I walk on Monday and Tuesday?"

6. For some of the missing words you have a choice of two or more. George *must* be your uncle since he is the husband of your aunt. Your aunt can be an *excellent* or an *admirable* hostess, but you cannot put in *good* or *wonderful* because of the word "an" just before the gap.

7. If you are in any doubt, write down the name of the days of the week, and you will see the answers for (*c*) and (*d*) at once.

8. Be careful with (*e*). It has nothing to do with a clock. Arrange the five drawings in your mind so that the change from one to the next is regular.

9. The important clue is the date on which the letter was written—Sunday, April 28th. It is best to write down the days of the week with their dates according to the calendar, from the previous Friday, April 26th, to the following Friday, May 3rd. Then the answers can be clearly seen.

10. By inference and elimination and careful study of the clues, this question can be answered. Write down the numbers 1, 2, 3, 4, 5. A tall man won, so it is either Brown or Smith. Green came in front of men he disliked, Smith and Jones, so it leaves Brown as number 1. Green is therefore number 2, and as we are told Jones was fourth, Smith must be third. White (a small man) is left for the fifth place.

GENERAL PAPER 5

1. In the passage below are many words that should not be there. Copy the passage, leaving these words out, so that it will read sensibly:

There is often was a heavy parcel shower of sunshine rain this in the afternoon. It finished started just hours after I must had left off school and then before I saw reached home I shall be was drenched. Mother made expected me to change iron all my clothes before as soon as I got arrived in the home. She said I shall should catch the a cold unless if I did had so.

2. Jack is now 16 years old. Four years ago he was twice as old as his sister.

   (a) How old was his sister four years ago?

   (b) How old is his sister now?

   (c) How old was Jack when she was born?

   (d) How old will Jack be when she is twice as old as he is now?

   (e) When will she and Jack be the same age at the same time?

3. Each of the small squares in this diagram has a special name.

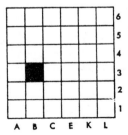

For example, the name of the shaded square is B3, since it is above the letter B and opposite the figure 3.

(a) Put a cross in the square K4.

(b) What is the name of the square in the top left-hand corner?

(c) What is the name of the square which is two squares to the left of the square which is two squares above L3?

(d) What is the name of the square which is one square above the square which is one square below the square which is two squares to the right of C3?

(e) If the direction from K4 to K3 is West, what is the direction from K4 to E4?

4. The following words can be arranged in pairs, so that the words in each pair are spelt with the same letters. Write out the pairs correctly.

STEAM	PLEAT	HEART
HEARS	REAPS	LEAPT
PLANE	SCARE	SPARE
STARE	SPATE	RATES
CHEAT	TEACH	SLATE
PEACH	SHARE	CHEAP
EARTH	PASTE	PANEL
LEAST	MATES	RACES

5. Complete the following patterns to the end of the line:

(a)

(b)

(c)

(d)

(e)

6. Arrange each list of words in alphabetical order.

   (*a*)   Smith   Jones   Stone   Jackson   Short   Sharp

   (*b*)   carry   cargo   catch   castle   car   carpet

   (*c*)   merry   bring   whale   draper   bright   night

   (*d*)   Margot   Mavis   May   Mary   Maisie   Margaret

   (*e*)   strong   strength   strap   stretch   street   strip

7. A farmer walked two miles due east and then turned and walked a mile due north. Next he turned to his right and walked in that direction. What direction was it—north, east, south or west?

8. In a bag there are ten counters numbered 1 to 10. A, B, C, D and E each drew out two counters and the sum of the numbers on their counters was as follows.

   A, 4: B, 7: C, 11: D, 16: E, 17.

   What actual numbers did each one draw?

9. In the following sentences you will see that some words are in brackets. Four words follow each sentence. One of these has the same, or nearly the same, meaning as the word in brackets. Write this word down.

   (*a*)   I bought a pane of (clear) glass.
        (distinct, transparent, frosted, tinted)

   (*b*)   An (accurate) answer is required.
        (correct, clear, neat, tidy)

   (*c*)   Uncle John was a (melancholy) man.
        (mean, surly, sad, poor)

(*d*) He was in receipt of a (substantial) income.
(firm, considerable, uncertain, meagre)

(*e*) The error was of no great (significance).
(handwriting, reality, importance, result)

(*f*) The majority of the people were (illiterate).
(careless, stupid, unable to speak, unable to read)

(*g*) A child's birthday is an (annual) occurrence.
(usual, yearly, exciting, happy)

(*h*) What (folly) to think that things will improve.
(stupidity, insight, wisdom, news)

(*i*) The package had been plainly marked (fragile).
(light, careful, brittle, thin)

(*j*) A metal bar will (contract) in cold weather.
(break, freeze, lengthen, shorten)

10. Mr. Brown never calls his relations by their correct names, but always in a roundabout way. Thus, he always calls himself, "My father's son." He has one sister, a father and mother and a grandfather and grandmother. He also has a son and a daughter. His wife has no relations but him and the children. Underline, on the right, which of his relations you think he means in each of the following expressions: —

My son's sister's father FATHER, GRANDFATHER, HIMSELF

My mother's husband's father's grandson FATHER, SON, HIMSELF

My wife's son's great grandfather HIMSELF, FATHER, GRAND-FATHER

My sister's father's son's wife WIFE, MOTHER, GRAND-MOTHER.

HINTS TO GENERAL PAPER 5

2. First find the present ages of Jack and his sister, and the difference in their ages. Jack, now 16, when 12, was twice as old as his sister; so she was then 6, and now is 10, so that there is a difference in their ages of 6 years. The answers to the various questions can then be worked out, except for (e). Here the answer must be "never", for as she is now 6 years younger than Jack, she must always remain so.

8. First write down the ten numbers, and as they are used strike them off the list. Begin with A. His total is four which can be made up of the possible groups—4 and 0; 3 and 1; 2 and 2. Only one solution, 3 and 1, is correct because there is no 0 and only one 2. The others can soon be worked out from the remaining numbers.

ANSWERS

ENGLISH PAPER 1

1. (a) PUPPY. FOAL. DUCKLING. (3)

   (b) WEALTHY. SAFE. RIGID. (3)

   (c) The two boys, boxing each other, tried too hard to win the fight. (3)

   (d) Norah said, "No. I can't come." (3)   (12 marks)

2. (a) Someone who is always willing to help his country is PATRIOTIC. (2)

   (b) Someone who refuses to change his mind is OBSTINATE. (2)

   (c) Someone who always behaves unpleasantly is ODIOUS. (2)

   (d) Someone who is lively and active is VIVACIOUS. (2)

   (e) Someone who looks on the bad side of things is PESSIMISTIC. (2)   (10 marks)

3. (a) The ladies were lifting their very heavy boxes. (3)

   (b) The men-servants were putting their masters' meals on the tables. (5)

   (c) "We are playing with our pet deer," said the boys. (*Not* deers.) (4)

   (d) The men's caps were blown off in the storms. (4)

   (e) The fires were burning brightly. (2)   (18 marks)

4. (a) Mr. and Mrs. Jones, whose son is called Owen, are Welsh.

   (b) Jack, my best friend, whom I have known for years, is in hospital.

   (c) The policeman stopped the small boy who was kicking a ball in the street.

   (d) The flowers which I saw on the table were lovely.

   (e) We could not see the girl for whom we were looking.
          (10 marks)

5. (a) The bed was probably a four-poster, because it had curtains around it. (2)

   (b) Miss Wentworth had lived there for sixty-six years. (1)

   (c) She was worried about the money she owed. (1)

   (d) No, she was not happy because she was worried. (1)

   (e) Two of the following:—big, old, curtained. (2)

   (f) She sold pigs, fruit, and vegetables. (3)

   (g) (i) She owed a lot of money, even though she had an allowance.

       (ii) The money she made from selling her produce made up only a very small part of the total money she owed to people.

       (iii) The house had been her home for so long it seemed as if she were married to it. (6)

   (h) She was looking for the moon and stars. (1)

   (i) Dim; haggard; contrive. (3)   (20 marks)

6. Letter.   (30 marks)
                          TOTAL:—   (100 marks)

ENGLISH PAPER 2

1. (a) "Can you lend me a suitcase?"
       "No, I can't," replied Mary. (4)

   (b) Jack and Henry did their work well although they went about it in a queer way. (4)

   (c) The two girls discussed what they should wear at the party if their friends were to invite them. (2)

   (d) The new girl in the dormitory knew that she would have to share her tuck with the older girls. (2)   (12 marks)

2. All the boys and girls wanted to have a fine day for their outing, when they were going by coach to a lovely seaside place. But, at first, it seemed as if it might rain, which was not pleasant at all, as they would not be able to see any beautiful views from the coach. Later the sun shone and it turned out a really sunny afternoon. They enjoyed their day on a sandy beach and then went to a green field for tea and sports.   (12 marks)

3. (a) The tramp tried to steal the steel box from the bank during the night.

   (b) During the storm the rains caused a leak in the roof of the old shed.

   (c) The mistress said, "All girls are to wear their blue blazers and to stand there this afternoon during the ceremony."

   (d) The judge said that the witch would be burnt at the stake.

   (e) Our friends did the whole journey in less than one hour.

   (14 marks)

4. (a) United Nations Organisation.

   (b) Cash on Delivery.

   (c) On Her Majesty's Service.

   (d) British Railways.

   (e) Please reply.
   (This is the translation of the French—
   Répondez s'il vous plaît.)

   (f) British Overseas Airways Corporation.   (12 marks)

5. (a) Spring is the time of the year, probably March.   (1)

   (b) Because the violets were growing.   (2)

   (c) Daphne was wearing a Chinese coat.   (1)

   (d) Orlando was a cat.   (2)

   (e) John was not anxious at the moment because his wife, Daphne, was happy.   (2)

   (f) Nimbus means a halo or circle of light.   (2)

   (g) (i) On the edge of the lit-up area.
   (ii) The light from the fire shone.   (4)

   (h) (i) scented; (ii) failure; (iii) cabinet. (6)   (20 marks)

6. Composition.   (30 marks)
                         TOTAL: (100 marks)

ENGLISH PAPER 3

1. (a) PRINCESS. WAITRESS. SULTANA. VIXEN. (4)

   (b) DIARIES. MICE. COURTS-MARTIAL. TOMATOES. (4)

   (c) Although the weather was fine, we could not decide whether to go across the moors or by the path. (1)

   (d) The child was left by its mother for four hours.

   We took the turning to the left, and soon arrived at our destination.

   As the load was light, the porter brought it to our train very quickly.

   On the next day, before it was light, the travellers set out.

   The girl showed her engagement ring to her friend.

   The visitor went to ring the bell again, as he was not heard the first time. (6)   (15 marks)

2. (a) Please come immediately.

   (b) I am innocent.

   (c) Yesterday I met a Frenchman.

   (d) This book was given to me by the author.

   (e) He was despised by many people because he was a miser.

   (f) The congregation listened attentively to the sermon.

   (g) The audience clapped.

   (h) Dentists can extract teeth painlessly.   (8 marks)

3.

EASY	DIFFICULT	(2)
LOVE	HATE	(2)
TRANSPARENT	OPAQUE	(2)
REFUSE	ACCEPT	(2)
CORRECT	WRONG	(2)
PROBABLE	UNLIKELY	(2)

(12 marks)

4. (*a*) The man ran quickly down the road. (*Adverb*)

   (*b*) We had a thrilling time at the sports. (*Adjective*)

   (*c*) The boys tried to climb over the gate to get into the field. (*Preposition*)

   (*d*) The maid baked a cake in the oven. (*Verb*)

   (*e*) John practised hard for his race, and so he won it. (*Conjunction*)

   (1 for each word and 2 for part of speech)   (15 marks)

5. (*a*) The Sydney Star was a ship. (1)

   (*b*) John was going to sea as a cadet. (1)

   (*c*) John had been living at Brixton. (1)

   (*d*) John's father was not rich, as he could "ill afford" the loss of a day's wages to take his son to the ship. (2)

   (*e*) She was cast down because she was sad at the thought of John going to sea. (2)

   (*f*) "cherished" shows that John liked his cap. (2)

   (*g*) John spoke respectfully to Mr. Davies, because he was an officer and superior to him. (2)

   (*h*) Mr. Brown was John's schoolmaster. (1)

   (*i*) John wore dungarees. (1)

   (*j*) Because he was pleased with it, and thought he might be able to use it later, but he realised he must concentrate on his present job first. (2)

   (*k*) fat. unwilling. (2)

   (*l*) That evening John went to look at his new knife. He received a shock, for he found that it was missing. He immediately thought of his room mate. He went to their cabin, and as the room was empty John searched the other cadet's box. He discovered the knife, concealed under some paper at the bottom. Later Roy, the other cadet, confessed that he had stolen the knife because he had lost his own. (3)

   (20 marks)

6. Letter.   (30 marks)

                      TOTAL: (100 marks)

ENGLISH PAPER 4

1. (a) The man was as deaf as a post.
      The old lady was as poor as a church mouse.
      The poor girl was as hungry as a hunter.   (3)

   (b) DANGEROUS.   DOUBTFUL.   BEAUTIFUL.   (3)

   (c) The score at the end of the game was 1—1, so it was a draw.
      The artist tried hard to draw the picture of the tree.
      The ship was known to draw seven feet of water when
      laden.   (3)

   (d) (i) Mr. & Mrs. W. Jones,
              4, High Street,
                 Exeter,
                    Devon.

       (ii) A. W. White, Esq.,
               Manor House,
                  Sibford,
                     Oxon.   (4)   (13 marks)

2. | HORSE | STABLE | RABBIT | BURROW |
   |---------|--------|--------|--------|
   | CHICKEN | COOP | PIG | STY |
   | COW | BYRE | FOX | LAIR |
   | DOG | KENNEL | SHEEP | FOLD |
   | BADGER | SETT | | (18 marks) |

3. (a) DENIED.   (b) CARELESS.   (c) LEGIBLE.

   (d) FORMER.   (e) DISPLEASED.   (f) SUCCESS.
                                              (12 marks)

4. (a) The girl was tired, so she went to lie down.

   (b) "I lay down yesterday," said Tom.

   (c) At our church last Sunday, the choir sang a new anthem.

(d) The choirboys said that they had sung the same hymn the previous Sunday.

(e) Neither of the boys was the winner.

(f) The headmaster wrote a good report for his prefect.

(g) The boy had written his name incorrectly.   (7 marks)

5. (a) Charlie was asked to ride a horse quickly to London.   (1)

   (b) He could have said that he had hardly ridden in his life.   (1)

   (c) A benefactor is one who has done some kindly deed or helped someone considerably.   (2)

   (d) "familiar".   (2)

   (e) "beloved".   (2)

   (f) faithful.   determined.

   (g) Obadiah was a stableman.   (1)

   (h) Charlie wanted a fast-trotting steed and Dobbin was too slow.   (1)

   (i) He could hold on by the mane, if necessary.   (1)

   (j) "Be careful to follow the motion of the horse. Whistle a tune according to the speed of the horse, and then move to its rhythm."   (3)

   (k) bidden, steed, highway are words not much used nowadays.   (3)

   (l) Charlie was ordered to "ride a horse to London".   (3)
                                                        (20 marks)

6. Composition.   (30 marks)
                          TOTAL: (100 marks)

ENGLISH PAPER 5

1. (a) (i) Tom and I did our homework quickly.
      (ii) Between you and me, I think the first of the two pictures is the better.
      (iii) None of the boys was in the classroom when the master came in. (6)

   (b) (i) I shall be going abroad next summer.
      (ii) The old lady fell over because the road was very slippery.
      (iii) The distance from my house to the hospital is about two miles. (3)

   (c)
I draw	I drew	I have drawn
I cry	I cried	I have cried
I write	I wrote	I have written
I choose	I chose	I have chosen
I lie (down)	I lay	I have lain (5)

   (d) The master said, "Who is talking?" (2)   (16 marks)

2. IMPATIENT. ILLEGIBLE. UNHAPPY. IMPOSSIBLE. INSECURE. DISOBEDIENT. UNABLE. INCORRECT. NONSENSE. DISAGREE.
                                                    (10 marks)

3. STAKE, STEAK. PEAR, PAIR (or PARE). FAIN, FEIGN. VALE, VEIL. LEAK, LEEK. READ, REED. RAZE, RAISE. FAIR, FARE. (10 marks)

4. Mrs. Smith went slowly down the road, trying to think of all she needed at the grocer's shop. Before she arrived there she met her friend, Mrs. Jones, and said to her, "Where are you going, dear?" Mrs. Jones said, "To the same shop as you, I expect," and they went on their way, arm-in-arm. (14 marks)

5. (a) Slipper was a sea-lion. (2)

   (b) Another name might be Flipper. (1)

   (c) Her mother was alarmed because Slipper was showing no signs of life. (2)

   (d) Slipper spent most of her first weeks sleeping and eating. (1)

   (e) "Taking a nap" means sleeping for a short while. (2)

   (f) The baby grew rapidly because it drank milk ten times as rich as cow's milk. (2)

   (g) Slipper felt terrified. (2)

   (h) "Helpless" means unable to do anything useful; "favourite" means the one that is liked best; "dangling" means hanging loosely; "twitching" means moving in a short, sudden manner. (8)   (20 marks)

6. Composition.   (30 marks)
                              TOTAL: (100 marks)

ARITHMETIC PAPER 1

1. (a) 684   (b) 60
    (c) £9.02   (d) 365
    (e) 2 700   (f) 20 000
    (g) 16, 22   (h) $\frac{1}{8}$, $\frac{2}{20}$, $1\frac{7}{8}$, $\frac{1}{2}$, $\frac{3}{8}$ (16 marks)

2. £18.54   (4 marks)

3. (a) 793   (b) 1 586   (6 marks)

4. £5.02   (6 marks)

5. 45p   (10 marks)

6. 81 366   (10 marks)

7. Father 90.25 kg; son 39.75 kg   (10 marks)

8. 4 min. 20 sec.   (8 marks)

9. $60\frac{1}{2}$p   (8 marks)

10. (a) 55 cm; 3 025 sq. cm   (8)
    (b) 8.60 m   (10)
    (c) 6   (4)   (22 marks)
                                TOTAL: (100 marks)

ARITHMETIC PAPER 2

1. (a) 2 661   (b) Yes
    (c) 0.775025   (d) 8
    (e) 6   (f) five million, four hundred
                                           and seven thousand and
                                           sixty eight
    (g) $2 \times 2 \times 3 \times 3 \times 5$ (h) 2p   (16 marks)

2.
	1 doz. eggs @ $2\frac{1}{2}$p each	£0.30
	$1\frac{1}{2}$ kg sugar @ 8p per kg	0.12
	1 pkt. cornflakes @ 8p	0.08
	2 jellies @ $4\frac{1}{2}$p each	0.09
	300 g cheese @ £1 per kg	0.30
	$\frac{1}{4}$ kg bacon @ 62p per kg	$0.15\frac{1}{2}$
	TOTAL:	£$1.04\frac{1}{2}$

                                                                 (8 marks)

3. 70p   (8 marks)

4. £1.42½   (6 marks)

5. (a) 7   (2)
    (b) 2 hours, 46 minutes, 40 seconds   (4)   (6 marks)

6. 32 pieces; 8 cm   (10 marks)

7. £4.65   (8 marks)

8. £1   (10 marks)

9. 6⅔ hours   (10 marks)

10. (a) 720   (5)
    (b) Cow £40; Horse £20; Pig £10   (7)
    (c) 975 sq. m   (6)   (18 marks)
                                    TOTAL: (100 marks)

ARITHMETIC PAPER 3

1. (a) 6 265   (b) 147
    (c) 293   (d) One
    (e) 2.160 km   (f) 7 500 sq. metres
    (g) 7.36 a.m.   (h) 615 g   (16 marks)

2. (a) 2 hours 19 min. 17 seconds
    (b) 48 min. per day   (8 marks)

3. £17.50   (6 marks)

4. 122 days   (6 marks)

5. 44 eggs   (6 marks)

6. 1½ cm   (8 marks)

7. 8¼ hours   (8 marks)

8. £13.65   (8 marks)

9. (a) 240 litres
    (b) 96 customers   (10 marks)

10. (a) (i) 90 seconds (ii) 40 km per hour   (8)
    (b) £60   (8)
    (c) 7   (8)   (24 marks)
                                    TOTAL: (100 marks)

ARITHMETIC PAPER 4

1. (a) $\frac{5}{8}$ (b) 2.25 (c) 125 g
   (d) 14 (e) 27 (f) 4 236
   (g) 40 (h) 8 hours 57 min. (16 marks)

2. 48 (8 marks)

3. £63.13$\frac{1}{2}$ (6 marks)

4. (a) 90p (b) 13p (6 marks)

5. (a) 174 (b) 17.4 (c) 137.27 (9 marks)

6. £66.84 (10 marks)

7. (a) 252 cm (b) No (5 marks)

8. 20 sec. past 4.31 p.m. (6 marks)

9. 3.2 km per hour (10 marks)

10. (a) 128 sq. metres (6)
    (b) 8 sheep from C to B, 11 sheep from B to A. (9)
    (c) 10 days. (9)
    (24 marks)
    TOTAL: (100 marks)

ARITHMETIC PAPER 5

1. (a) 752 (b) 684 (c) 9
   (d) 47$\frac{1}{2}$p (e) 1 hour 52 min. (f) 2.225 kg
   (g) 112 minutes (h) 3 996 (16 marks)

2. (a) 144 (b) 41 (4 marks)

3. 40 (4 marks)

4. $\frac{8}{32}$ (10 marks)

5. 38$\frac{1}{2}$p (10 marks)

6. 112.5 metres (12 marks)

7. 50p (8 marks)

8. Four (8 marks)

9. 104 (12 marks)

10. (a) 134 pages (4)
    (b) 8$\frac{1}{2}$p; 52 letters (6)
    (c) £2 (6) (16 marks)
    TOTAL: (100 marks)

GENERAL PAPER 1

1. (a) 14 years   (b) oak, beech   (8 marks)

2. tidy, foreword, place, throng, contain, unit, pair, recent, fierce, fourth.   (10 marks)

3. $\frac{1}{10}$ kg,   5 cubic cm,   0.5 g, $\frac{1}{100}$ kg.   (4 marks)

4. (a) M (monkey)   (b) A (adder)   (c) L (lizard)
   (d) E (elephant)   (e) S (sheep)   (f) G (giraffe)
   (g) R (rabbit)   (h) O (otter)   (i) W (walrus)
   (j) L (leopard).

                (10 marks)

5. 5   (4 marks)

6. COAT, COST, HOST   (6 marks)

7. (a) A bird in the hand is worth two in the bush.
   (b) A stitch in time saves nine.
   (c) Too many cooks spoil the broth.
   (d) A rolling stone gathers no moss.
   (e) Out of sight, out of mind.   (10 marks)

8. (a) $8 + 3 \times 10 = 38$
   (b) $2 \times 12 \div 4 = 6$
   (c) $5 + 7 - 3 = 9$
   (d) $11 - 6 + 9 = 14$
   (e) $4 \times 5 - 6 = 14$ (15 marks)

9.
the Atlantic alone in a rubber	3
that shipwrecked men can live	8
scientist who is attempting to cross	2
for a long time on fish.	9
terday at three o'clock. He left his	5
Dr. Alan Bombard, a French	1
Tangier. He is trying to prove	7
boat, sailed into Casablanca yes	4
mate and navigator behind at	6

                (18 marks)

	Alice	Mary	Maud	No-one
10. (a)		✓		
(b)				✓
(c)	✓			
(d)				✓
(e)			✓	

                (15 marks)

TOTAL: (100 marks)

GENERAL PAPER 2

1. (*a*) I X X K   (*b*) M X L X   (*c*) N O X X
   (*d*) O T X U   (*e*) O E X P   (15 marks)

2. London is the capital of England.
   (*or*: The capital of England is London)
   She slipped and fell down the stairs.
   The girl saw the two motor-cars bump each other.
   The lion roared and the man fired his gun.
   The bus stopped and the child got off.   (10 marks)

3. (*a*) Y   (*b*) A   (*c*) R   (*d*) D
   (*e*) L   (*f*) E   (*g*) N   (*h*) G
   (*i*) T   (*j*) H   (10 marks)

4. PUT, CORN, ACORN, BENT, SKEWER, STATION   (6 marks)

5. COME AND BRING SOME HELP QUICKLY.   (5 marks)

6. (*a*) 18.
   (*b*) If, instead, Rose had given Gwen 2p, then
   Gwen would have had 8p more than Rose.   (8 marks)

7. (*a*) K   (*b*) K   (*c*) M   (*d*) Q   (*e*) O   (10 marks)

8. (*a*) HI   (*b*) THERE   (*c*) 36   (*d*) WOMAN
   (*e*) CONSTELLATION   (*f*) MOTHER   (*g*) COME
   (*h*) BEEF   (*i*) DISTANCE   (*j*) NOWHERE   (10 marks)

9. (*a*) 2   (*b*) 3   (*c*) 2   (*d*) 2
   (*e*) 2   (*f*) 1   (*g*) 2   (14 marks)

10.

1	6	5
8	2	9
4	7	3

                        (12 marks)

TOTAL: (100 marks)

GENERAL PAPER 3

1. (a) 103   (b) Saturday   (c) 34   (d) rings
   (e) Monday   (10 marks)

2. door, umbrella, clock (watch), pilot, shears, orchard.   (12 marks)

3. (a) No   (b) Yes   (c) No   (d) No   (e) No   (5 marks)
   (Answer to (e) = "No, I am not sure.")

4. PRIM, PLUM, SOLE, SURE, PALM, SAFE, SATE   (7 marks)

5. Tom — 10, John — 14.   (5 marks)

6. (a) I   (b) O   (c) H   (d) O   (e) R   (10 marks)

7. (1) D (2) E (3) A (4) D (5) E (6) A   (12 marks)

8. (a) GREEN   (b) LESS   (c) PLANE   (d) KNOCK
   (e) BLOTS   (f) LONGEST   (g) EXPAND
   (h) FREEZE   (i) DRY   (j) STARCH   (10 marks)

9. (a) Peter   (b) Jack   (c) Susan   (d) Doris
   (e) Susan   (f) Mary, Peter   (g) Arithmetic   (14 marks)

10.

1	George	SMITH	*Plumber*
3	Tom	BROWN	*Solicitor*
5	Fred	FARRAR	*Furrier*
7	Bert	JONES	*Merchant*
9	Arthur	AMBLER	*Auctioneer*

(15 marks)

TOTAL: (100 marks)

GENERAL PAPER 4

1. (*a*) TULIP (*b*) UMBRELLA (*c*) PAPER (*d*) RIDE
   (*e*) LARD (*f*) POTATO (*g*) CRAB (*h*) BUGLER (8 marks)

2. (*a*) P (*b*) R (*c*) O (*d*) M (*e*) E
   (*f*) N (*g*) A (*h*) N (*i*) E (*j*) S (10 marks)

3. C (10 marks)

4. (*a*) 64, 128 (*b*) 43, 50 (*c*) 33, 28
   (*d*) 23, 30 (*e*) 5, 12 (*f*) 729, 2 187
   (*g*) 15, 6 (*h*) 17, 23 (16 marks)

5. Sunday (5 marks)

6. uncle, house (cottage), stay, forward, excellent,
   feel, clean, feed, mow. (9 marks)

7. (*a*) I (*b*) Since (*c*) Sunday, Tuesday
   (*d*) Sunday, Monday, Friday (*e*) A, T (5 marks)

8. (*a*) WHITEHALL, AUSTRALIA.
   (*b*) POOR, EXCELLENT.
   (*c*) EGG-CUP, RESERVOIR.
   (*d*) ●●●●——   ——●●●●

   (*e*) (*f*) YEAR, HOUR.

   First and last interchangeable. (12 marks)

9. (*a*) April 26th (*b*) May 1st (*c*) May 3rd
   (*d*) Wednesday (*e*) 5 (10 marks)

10. 1st BROWN, 2nd GREEN, 3rd SMITH,
    4th JONES, 5th WHITE. (15 marks)
    TOTAL: (100 marks)

GENERAL PAPER 5

1. There was a heavy shower of rain this afternoon. It started just after I had left school and before I reached home I was drenched. Mother made me change all my clothes as soon as I arrived home. She said I should catch a cold unless I did so. (10 marks)

2. (*a*) 6   (*b*) 10   (*c*) 6   (*d*) 38   (*e*) never. (10 marks)

3. (*b*) A6   (*c*) E5   (*d*) K3   (*e*) North (10 marks)

4. STEAM, MATES; LEAST, SLATE; PLANE, PANEL;
STARE, RATES; SHARE, HEARS; EARTH, HEART;
CHEAT, TEACH; CHEAP, PEACH; PLEAT, LEAPT;
REAPS, SPARE; SPATE, PASTE; SCARE, RACES. (12 marks)

5. (*a*)   (*b*)   (*c*)   (*d*)   (*e*)

(15 marks)

6. (*a*) Jackson, Jones, Sharp, Short, Smith, Stone.
(*b*) car, cargo, carpet, carry, castle, catch.
(*c*) bright, bring, draper, merry, night, whale.
(*d*) Maisie, Margaret, Margot, Mary, Mavis, May.
(*e*) strap, street, strength, stretch, strip, strong. (10 marks)

7. EAST. (5 marks)

8. A — 1, 3;   B — 5, 2;   C — 7, 4;
D — 10, 6;   E — 9, 8. (10 marks)

9. (*a*) transparent   (*b*) correct
(*c*) sad   (*d*) considerable
(*e*) importance   (*f*) unable to read
(*g*) yearly   (*h*) stupidity
(*i*) brittle   (*j*) shorten (10 marks)

10. himself   himself   grandfather   wife (8 marks)
                    TOTAL: (100 marks)

Name:..   Form:....................

PROGRESS SHEET

Test	Time	Marks
English Paper 1	....	....
English Paper 2	....	....
English Paper 3	....	....
English Paper 4	....	....
English Paper 5	....	....
General Paper 1	....	....
General Paper 2	....	....
General Paper 3	....	....
General Paper 4	....	....
General Paper 5	....	....
Arithmetic Paper 1	....	....
Arithmetic Paper 2	....	....
Arithmetic Paper 3	....	....
Arithmetic Paper 4	....	....
Arithmetic Paper 5	....	....